21st Century Fox
Space Age Pimping

By
Paradise

Infinite Dreams
Publishing

Published by
Infinite Dreams
Great Britain
infinitedreamspublishing@gmail.com

Text and Art copyright © 2001 by Infinite Dreams
First Edition Published 2001

ISBN 09541355-0-4

The publisher would like to thank The Kidd, El Bandido and Topchoice.

Cover art by One Black Dog. Concept by Paradise.

Dedication

To those who are truly free. Who are masters of their living present, therefore the masters of their destiny and past.

Acknowledgement

This is the book I never had, and always wanted. I wish I'd been able to read it when I was seventeen.

I'd like to acknowledge all the thoroughbred hoes that unknowingly schooled me through Pimp kindergarten, Pimp University and beyond. Who gave me that personal tuition until I graduated with my PhD: Pimpin' hoes Degree.

I would like to acknowledge Iceberg Slim's influence on my thinking. Through his eminent skills as a writer, as a seeker of the truth – no matter if bitter or sweet - and as a man with soul.

Concrete respect to my brother from a different mother, The Kidd! The influence of his knowledge on mine speaks volumes by its presence, particularly in the "Procurement" section of the book. Through both our knowledge, others will cheat time too. It's all good.

Respect to El Bandido for making many things possible.

Finally, I wish to acknowledge the enthusiasm and respect I have received from my friends in the United States, Canada, Europe and my own country of England. My respect and enthusiasm are with you also.

Contents

Preface

In an idyllic world, this book would not exist.

Who you are would take precedence over what you are superficially. People would place importance in being themselves with one another. Men and women would act with as much respect towards each other as they have for themselves. They would follow the ethic that Confucius advised: to do to others as you would wish done to yourself. But let's flip back to reality.

In reality, there are many men and women who have relationships which are not pure. By their own design.

These people will be playing one of three different types of roles: trick, hoe, or Pimp.

Hoes are people who consider status, material possessions and wealth important when it comes to relationships. The name trick is applicable to any person who rewards a hoe with status, possessions or wealth for sexual reasons.

Everyone I meet, I judge by their own actions and words. I treat people appropriately. I treat a true friend accordingly. I treat a hoe accordingly. And I can tell a hoe faster than I can boil an egg. Without hoes there cannot be Pimps. And without tricks there can't be hoes. Just a thought.

This book is simply a glimpse into part of my world. I have written it with two aims in mind. It is as much an examination of my own studies of human behaviour, psychology and my philosophies as it is a bible to someone who would want to use its contents practically.

It is intended to provoke thought, discussion, debate and innovation, rather than waste ink attempting to convert people to my viewpoint, glamorising, being self-important or treading water justifying myself defensively. So what some will acclaim to be the virtue of this book makes it less accessible to many. We're going to start off at the deep-end and then submerge down deep as the Atlantic Trench. The descent will be strange and uncomfortable to those who have never dived before, but fascinating to those with a little "Jacques Cousteau" in their blood.

So whether you are inquisitive, enjoy insight into someone else's mind, or wish to examine your own opinions - if only to confirm them - be my welcome guest and read on. But this book is for those who, like I, feel what we refer to as "the Force" flowing strong within them.

Introduction

*Explain the game? It's like talking
astrophysics to a motherfuckin' wino.*
Rosebudd

Being a 21st Century Fox means being able to interact
with *anyone* without being taken advantage of.

This implies having an understanding of reality:
knowing the forces that influence everything that
happens in relationships. It also implies understanding
what type of person someone is, so that I can decide to
interact with them or not. This decision is not influenced
by fear of being taken advantage of, because there is
none. It can't happen.

But why would anyone decide to interact with the hoe
type of person, even in the absence of fear of, and
absence of, exploitation?

For any reason at all, so long as it does not require a
judgment of the other person's ethics.

I do know that some men and women find themselves
in a situation where they do not wish to, or no longer
wish to, cut themselves off from experiencing the
company of others, intimacy, or having fun and
excitement, just because there is nobody that they
would define as having honourable intentions available.

A Fox understands that what a person will do given
free reign and unlimited power will reflect their ethics,
but that is different to what that person will do when
they are not given this liberty. Maybe you have observed
how a child can behave like a little angel around one
parent and misbehave and run rings around the other?
Perhaps you recognise that how you will behave in a
church, or with a police officer, or during a job interview,
or with your surgeon, is significantly different to how you
interact with a checkout operator, a friend, a small child,
your grandfather, or someone you dislike.

So if I'm not engaging in what we might call a
"perfect" or "pure" relationship, being a 21st Century Fox
means safely entering the trick-hoe-Pimp world where

11

people will be tricky, will play games, and will take advantage, *if* they are enabled to do so!

So I am concerned with getting what I want behaviour-wise, from certain members of the opposite sex. It's about Power. It's about being myself. It's about applying aspects of Pimping to everyday situations. Reversing game on hoes. Only doing it many, many times more powerfully.

Why the interest in the Pimp definitions and psychology? In addition to drawing on our personal experiences, extensive observations, and substantial discussions, the Kidd and I have studied the most effective real-life examples of dealing effectively with manipulative people in relationships that we could find.

Some of the most useful, proven and advanced information, and terminology, that we have found has come from people, or books, concerned with the symbiotic relationship triangle of the Pimp, hoe and trick in some instances the underworld.

The word Pimp is thrown about in mainstream society, usually with little or no reference to its meaning. It is misused as a boast for someone who has sexual relationships with numerous women, liars, con men, woman-beaters, men of exceptional sexual prowess or low-down street scum. Or distorted by one-dimensional jokers with classic retro imagery of Cadillacs, fur coats and other wild paraphernalia. Pimps are also subject to unobjective coverage, negative stereotyping and misconceptions perpetuated through the media of film, news and music.

Unfortunately some Pimps con, harm, or threaten their hoes or hook them on drugs, but that isn't what makes them a Pimp. Just like a woman doesn't have to stand on a corner, or carry out a sexual act for money to be a hoe. Neither does a man need to be an escort or prostitute to be a hoe.

Substantial, real, contemporary information relating to the meaning of these words, if it does exist, is scarce. And that is exactly what you now hold in your hands.

Pimps can be found in cities all over the globe. Their means to their ends as individual as their personalities. A Pimp defined in a physical sense is someone who, regardless of their sex, race, age or method, receives money from a prostitute, a hoe. When I define a Pimp, I'm coming from a mental aspect. I am referring to a skilled individual who possesses and executes knowledge on hoes, which results in desired Behaviour and financial security. An effective manager. A master of counter-manipulation.

Now manipulation is not a always a negative term. Only the objective of manipulation that can be determined as good or bad; ethical, or not. The meaning of manipulation is "to use skilfully, to manage a person or situation to one's own advantage." This is any employer or manager's role. It applies to most human interaction. In my eyes, a real Pimp is a man or woman who controls a hoe's mind, and therefore controls everything else. Irrelevant of any other aspect of either person's life. This is what I call being a 21st Century Fox. It's being smart and using the best available technology. I get the benefits of a Pimp-type of psychology applied to in my everyday mainstream society surroundings, but I do not use it for illegal or unethical objectives.

A leader is a man who has the ability to get other people to do what they don't want to do, and like it.
Harry Truman

Not only will I take you through my entire process of dealing with hoes on a practical level, rich with specific, genuine examples and anecdotes. I will lay down my fundamental principles, concepts, and the psychological reasoning behind them. Because of this, you will have insight into my thoughts and paradigms and see how they are concrete, backing up my actions. You will understand the Power and control that I possess in my relationships.

Most importantly, you will be able to tailor this knowledge to your own requirements, build on it and innovate. Every artist uses their own unique methods and styles to obtain their required result. Being a 21st Century Fox is a living art form. I am still learning and innovating. A true Fox never stops.

Everything you are going to read is only my opinion.

13

The strongest opinion is one that is always open to question. A "Real Man" or woman, follows his or her own conscience. I welcome debate, feedback, contribution to, and the questioning of all information herein. I want you to think about this shit! Before you peel back the page, I'd like to say that arranging the contents of my mind into a logical sequential order of Copping, Tightening and Advanced has meant that many chapters overlap and interlock. So the book as a whole must be read in order for each of its units to be fully understood. Iceberg used to say that Pimping is like a watchmaker's art: its simple outer results belie its intricate inner mechanics of innumerable wheels within wheels.

Being a Real Man

*What shall it profit a man, if he shall gain
the whole world, and loose his soul?*
Mark 8:36

Although to the casual observer Pimping appears to result in shallow material gains, like a hoe, a master Pimp requires a deep understanding of the world and himself. Unlike a hoe, he places importance only on being in control, not on money, or anything else for that matter. He is at one with the tragic, yet beautiful "Laws of Reality." He is a psychologist. He follows his own conscience and, unlike a hoe, stays true to himself and other deserving people. He has strong principles, self-discipline and confidence. He knows what he desires. All of these virtues render him eminently desirable.

Before we get knee-deep in the practical side of being a Fox, I'd like to give you a broader sense of some of my inner thoughts, perceptions, principles and objectives. They are as crucial as the foundations to the Petronas Towers. This will help you understand my writings better.

*There is no duty we so much underrate
as the duty of being happy.*
Robert Louis Stevenson

My name isn't Paradise just because I like those dark chocolate coconut bars! What does that word conjure up in your mind? Chilling, fabulously unstressed, grinning like a Cheshire cat, resting on Egyptian cotton towels (a gift from a friend) on the terrace of a villa? Surveying the flawless talcum powder beach that declines into rippling bubble-bath turquoise sea as you reminisce last night's party, packed with your best friends? Enjoying the sunrays soaking into the Hawaiian Tropic a Coca-Cola mamacita has massaged all over you with equal enthusiasm as she has for using her initiative to spoil you? Now that's what I'm all about. Being happy. Living each and every day of my life as close to my vision of paradise as possible. Moving to make tomorrow come even closer to it.

Happiness is not directly dependent on wealth: it is directly dependent on your expectations.

Happiness is also obviously dependent on more than money, because you can be wealthy and lead a very unhappy life. We want to avoid painful divorces, fucked up relationships, lies to hide, vulnerability in our emotional expectations and so on. We require low stress, financial stability, and to have control, to be happy.

A second point to make on the subject of money and happiness is that a sunset or night sky does not look any better if you are a millionaire. An Egyptian cotton towel is affordable and feels just as nice if you are wealthy, or have below average income. A walk in the countryside, a snorkel in the sea, or strolling barefoot along a sandy beach are not affected by a bank balance. Neither does fresh-squeezed fruit juice, Cola, or good ice-cream taste better if you are a billionaire. Things like laughing with friends, receiving a warm hug, or going to a theme park are no better or more accessible if you are wealthy, or a just regular girl or guy.

Most importantly, my happiness is generated from an internal aspect: always enjoying the living present, relaxing, having fun, growing and being happy within, wherever I may be, or however wealthy I am.

I have a forty minute journey to work each day. I take advantage of it: enjoy the drive, take in the view, reflect, listen to music or audio books. I don't get mad, just like I don't get angry at, or expect to change, a hoe from being a hoe. That's as futile and illogical as getting mad at the sun setting every night. I expect it to set and it causes me no grief! I plan may actions accordingly. I'd make myself unhappy by expecting it not to set!

So I don't linger on the negative aspects of the universe. I use them to my benefit. All problems exist inside people's heads, not outside. The contents of many people's cerebrums don't acknowledge the Laws of Reality: truths that we aren't taught at school, but that are as relevant to us as gravity. It's like they're driving around on the wrong side of the road.

Another thing I do, but consider less important, is surround myself externally with the best company and environments possible.

Lastly, and least importantly, I surround myself with the best material items I can without debt, diminishing my ability to invest and save, or compromising my financial security. This ethos encompasses every aspect of my life. I never have and never will compromise on anything from hoes, to clothes, to toilet rolls.

My ultimate paradise will be when I have the financial freedom to use my time as I wish, to pursue my interests, socialise, learn, have fun, travel, not to sell it to an employer. To have my money work for me - not me for it. Because I'm all about making my world velvet, my relationships with women therefore must always be of a positive nature to these three ends. True friends enrich each other's lives in invaluable ways: inner qualities are unique and priceless. Whereas hoes are only as precious as the what value they contribute to a relationship. Money has its value stamped on it. Time, manners, gifts and effort are also valuable. This, and ethical behaviour, are the only justification hoes have to be allowed to deal with me. This philosophy, like the quote heading this chapter, is the definitive distinction between a hoe and I. My soul, my values, my Power are not for sale. This is one of several reasons why a hoe's Power is like rubbing a couple of twigs together, whilst I should be wearing nuclear hazard stickers.

As soon as you look for genuine love, friendship or trust in a hoe, you are loosing touch with reality. I've not put my heart on ice though. I'm sensitive and deep; I don't repress my feelings. I cry at the movies! It's because I'm so conscious that a hoe is incapable of provoking deeper feelings in me. Remember: to hoes everyone is either a trick or a treat (a Pimp). It's either, or. Therefore I have no hesitation putting my desires first and last when dealing with a hoe. I mean, she's already getting the treat of her life being in my presence - if I was a hoe, *I'd* want my number, you know! This management, this confidence, takes principles and knowledge. If someone tries to coerce you to do something you aren't comfortable with, you should have no qualms about saying so. Hoes don't give respect, nor will they let you earn it like real friends would. It must be enforced.

Hoes value the fact that I don't bend over to please them, or coerce them. They are accustomed to spineless tricks who they can manipulate. I stand out. Although I can come across self-centred, which is common ground anyway, they know I'm just being real with them. That it's the truth. They're complimented I even spend time with them because I use my time how it serves me best.

What can be more desirable than a man who deals with more than one woman, is honest with them, and they still deal with him?
The Kidd

A fool and his words are soon parted. Staying true to myself also includes the fact that I am honest, sincere and keep my word with people. I have come across many people not worth knowing, but never come across anyone "worth" lying to. This is how I have always been. People who are false pay the ultimate penalty. They waste their own lifetime. My time is not an unlimited resource!

Society is full of actors. Whether it's at work, socialising or pulling, it's all the same. Players, hoes and tricks lie. A "player" might think he's slick having several women. But they like who they *think* he is. And he has to keep propping up his house of cards. Then, inevitably, the truth will make itself known and it will tumble down.

I always tell the truth and am a man of principles. My women respect me for it. They desire me. They believe in me. They trust me. If I told them that they needed to wear shades at night they would do. They know that anything I say is for real. Good or bad, it's all good. Deceit is a sign of weakness, insecurity, disrespect and fear.

There is only one thing worse than being talked about, and that is not being talked about.
Oscar Wilde

When someone is successful, especially in relationships, business, and materially, it really brings the "haters" out of the woodwork. These are insecure, fearful wretches, like those three "friends" of Edmund in the Count of Monte Cristo. They want to put a spanner in the works, or try to latch onto me like a groupie, but detest me behind my back.

A hater will look at my happiness, the woman I'm with, my clothes, or car, and all he will see are things he hasn't got. He (or she) wants to scratch nice cars, accidentally-on-purpose spill a drink on someone, or spread rumours. By doing so, the hater uses some power, that in his own twisted way, he needs to assure himself of. Or he gets some satisfaction from drawing attention to himself and, therefore away from others. People who crave attention do not mind if it's negative or positive.

So the hater will look around and see his own fear and failure. He'll see me as a threat to him, sexually and egoistically. He's so insecure, he wishes everyone else was driving around in rusty buckets. I don't think like that. When I see someone with a mint girl, or gliding in a glossy Maserati, I'm happy for them. I'm glad they're successful. The world is a better place. It's cool to see. I'm inspired.

As a Fox You have to be self assured and greet the reaction of haters as confirmation of your success and - apparently - enviable qualities.

Insecure people are concerned with what badge people see on their car, not the feeling inside. They shop for anything they can afford with the largest, most blatant motif on it. They make their decisions in life based upon what society will think of them. Seeing me successful doing what I want, both socially and in business, hits a nerve. What I bear in mind is that people only talk about you if you are "valuable." In the media, coverage of celebrities' personal affairs sells, especially if bad. The bigger the star, the more coverage. The more they try and squeeze a scandal or sensation out of the most mundane event. It's a barometer of one's success. It comes with the territory.

When someone doesn't like me, or I dislike them, fine, it's a big world. Better than wasting time pretending. No two people agree on everything. I don't seek approval, nor do I fear disapproval. A Real Man or woman follows his or her own conscience. I would rather be hated for who I am, than be loved for who I'm not. Loved by few, hated by many. Like The Kidd says, "sometimes I look in the mirror and I even hate myself!"

To live happy, you have to be able to have a laugh at many so-called serious problems and have the understanding, confidence, and generosity, to allow them to be *other* people's problems!

Confidence is the greatest aphrodisiac. Overconfidence is a turnoff. It must be handled like nitro.
Ice-T

I strongly believe in myself. I have a good degree of confidence and bravado. This enables me to be more Powerful, because in addition to understanding the Laws of Reality, ego, insecurity and fear are the main deterrents preventing most people from realising their true potential.

Genuine confidence is balanced because it's free of insecurity. Some people with low self-esteem will appear and act over-the-top to try to compensate. Others will simply look and carry themselves under-confidently.

Insecurity is yet another reason a hoe is flawed compared to me. Although you'll catch me exclaiming things like I nearly wrecked my car looking at my own ice, my feet are firmly on the ground. I know that there is someone for everyone, and everyone for no one.

Consumer culture teaches the lemmings to look for happiness and affirmation of themselves exclusively externally. That everyone, or specific people, should like us, otherwise we're not cool. I don't over-rely on other people's approval to confirm my own value - although thousands can't be wrong! It's secondary to my own opinion. I'm sure you're familiar with a scenario where a friend is raving over an actor or actress, yet you don't know what the big deal is. Many people can't handle rejection, yet this truth seems perfectly logical and palatable if I use musical taste as a metaphor. To one

20

person a CD may be a corker; the next person wouldn't use it as a coaster. Neither is right or wrong.

Child-like insecurity, envy, jealousy and possessiveness are also prevalent in society when it comes to relationships, sex and Intimacy. People often use deception because they fear if they expose their true self they will not be approved of. Whereas my relationships are based on positive forces, effective methods and good ethics. A Real Man will say what he's doing and gain respect from it. I let women know what their, and my, status is, so there is no reasonable or acceptable reason to have problems in that area.

So, for example, if I am not in an exclusive relationship, girls regard me as single. If we spend a night together they are not given the impression that it is a change of status for us. A hoe has no say over what I do with my life or my body any more than I do over hers.

When your average person goes on a first date, they aren't going to start tripping off who each other was last intimate with. It's irrelevant. In the same way, a girl who dates me irregularly has no good reason to be concerned what I do with my time. Sexual activity is not the focus or basis of my relationships. It's quite the opposite! It's not really their business. But as with any good friends, I speak honestly and openly (but not graphically), according to how well I know them, if questioned about other women, intimacy, what I like about them, or when we last saw each other. Jealousy is not a turnoff: it's a motivation.

Private victories precede public victories. If you want the secondary greatness of recognition, focus first on primary greatness of character.
Stephen R Covey

The Balance of Power

*Nothing has more power over us than that
which we give it through our thoughts.*
Anthony Robbins

In the film of the same title, Neo first has to become
conscious that the "Matrix" exists. Then he learns how it
operates, how it is programmed, its rules, its flaws. It is
only when he understands it, that he is able to use this
knowledge to his own advantage. To overcome its mind-
blowing scale, unlearn, adapt his psyche to it,
manipulate it and do what he was previously conditioned
to think was impossible. Leap buildings! Bend spoons!
Dodge bullets! Walk through walls! Become invulnerable
to the Matrix.

Likewise, to wake you up to a few more essential
fundamentals that enable me to be a Fox, in the
following essays I will begin to unravel some of what my
American counterpart, The Kidd, refers to as "The
Matrix" that's all around us.

Since younger than we can remember, we all have
been constantly bombarded with information that
influences our perceptions of relationships, Behaviour
and protocol with the opposite sex. Whether it is tell-lie-
vision, cinema, magazines, toys, music, observation of
other people's social Behaviour, or advice from relatives.
The whole world is telling women to Pimp or hoe and
men to trick by conforming to these stereotypical
images. In fact, women have been given a free licence to
Pimp by society. It is socially acceptable for them to. If a
friend of the same sex acted in the same manner with
you, you would soon tell them where to go and what to
do! Females are conditioned to be comparatively vain,
invest in themselves and pay attention to their
appearance from childhood. The Matrix deters women
from overtly promiscuous Behaviour via a jealousy
system that will label them hoes and sluts, and via the
influence of certain religions. In Christianity, for
example, Mary's virgin birth is described as the

23

"Immaculate Conception." Immaculate meaning perfectly clean, free from fault, innocent, therefore tainting sexual intercourse. Society's message to men seems to be to treat women with respect at all times. No matter how bad they treat you, disregard it. Mothers tell their daughters, "Make sure he's got a good job." And is there a women's glossy that hasn't published an article on "How to Marry a Millionaire?" Walk into the average bookstore and you will find a wheelbarrow load of books on rules and techniques for manipulating men for questionable motives: books like "The Rules" which is so successful that it has sequels and reprints.

Hoes and tricks continually perpetuate that "ladies first" fallacy. Men are making the first move; offering drinks; wining and dining women; calling them up; chasing them; making up; buying jewellery; weekend breaks; on their knees proposing; not asking for prenuptials; abandoning financial security; throwing their jackets in puddles. Endeavouring to meet women's needs. Trying to prove their "love." Outright lying or paying for sex. Going to all kinds of lengths over women. But why?

Whatever you have heard about this being a man's world, forget it! When it comes to manipulation, women are gold medallists and men paraplegics. Who needs to own ninety percent of the world when the owner is your bitch? Who needs to be physically stronger when the law protects you? Who needs a seven, six, or even five-digit salary when some trick is going to do all the work for you and then let you spend it? Even ask you to spend it. And if you feel like splitting, you can take half of what they have earned with you. It is a stone cold fact that women have the winning knockout punch. Pussy. This, coupled with men's lack of sexual patience, is the single most influential factor in the Matrix. This means women are natural born Pimps, if they opt to be, and men are easily turned out into tricks. Actually they probably already were.

So generally, due to male desires and women's attributes, the female holds what I call the "Balance of Power." She is in control. The female is in more demand than the male. She can act passively and the male assumes a chasing role. Her vanity spirals off into the stratosphere! Thus, she can kick that "What have you done for me lately?" shit and demand certain Behaviour. Anything from buying her a drink to monogamous or open relationships, stable career, restrictions on the man's social life, favours, children, no children, generosity and gifts, to not leaving the toilet seat up! Whatever they choose that has to be complied with before they will let a man progress with them. The male tries to qualify, conform to the female's demands in order that she accepts him. Then he can fulfil his desires.

However, I remove the aforementioned sexual impatience and I'm effectively pulling the plug on their Balance of Power. Watch it drain down the plughole! It flows down the tube, straight into my tank! Now I'm not saying we're never going to crease sheets. Women want to have sex at least as much as men, but they get offered sex three hundred and sixty-five days a year. In fact by doing this, I'm heightening the hoe's desire for me, and eventually the hardest thing will be to keep her from indecently assaulting me. More on this later. A Fox thinks with his head, a trick lets his genitals make the decisions. I look at it from a mature perspective that I know is effective. Sex is not rare, it is not the objective of a relationship, it doesn't impress me. You can get it anywhere, any time if you really wanted to. A guy doesn't become a Haute Cuisine chef so that he can eat fantastic meals all day long! Now for the real knockout punch. Take the above strategy, keep it shut in that dark closet under the stairs, feed it steroids and growth hormones, mutate it, slap it about a bit and you get the real monster hoe Power drainer...

A true Fox doesn't need a hoe for A N Y T H I N G. Not for money, sex, friendship, not emotionally, nothing at all.

This may seem paradoxical, as the stereotypical Pimp image is that of someone who is dependent upon the income from his hoes, and receiving hoe's money is what the game is about. But this attitude is precisely what gives the ability to have Power. If I'm dependant on her in some way, then I'm afraid of loosing her, meaning I'm afraid of the consequences of my actions, meaning I'm not in control of her. Where does the Balance of Power lay? Would the employees of a company conduct themselves in the same manner as they did previously, upon discovering that their employer could never dismiss them?

Who would not want to be in a position where their hoe, or hoes, are able to support them well enough to sustain the life of a gentleman of leisure. But, for example, if I cannot support myself or visualise my life without a hoe, then they aren't dispensable to me like they should be. And how could I be dependent in any way on a gold-digging, deceitful, exploitative, materialistic, self-centred, untrustworthy, disrespectful, fronting, sexist hoe? I could bluff, front all I liked, but I would falter when she tested me out. Where true Power derives from is wanting her if she's cool with me, but not needing her if she's *not*.

Being relatively contented, indifferent, wanting, not needing all of the above things actually means I am more likely to obtain and retain a relationship. Knowing this and seeing it happen in practice makes it all the easier. Also, once you have women you're already intimate with, you aren't in any big hurry to get with your latest fan.

Hoes are as unaccustomed to having no Power as much as men are to having it. The Balance of Power can be given away in milliseconds. Milliseconds I tell you! Take tricks staring at a woman's body for instance. Looking at a girl and she catches you from the corner of her eye? You look guilty, then look away? Zap! Winking, using over-familiar language and grinning at women. Zap! Offer a drink. Zap! Tell her she looks gorgeous? Zap! Not being able to defuse outrageous sexual advances nonchalantly. Asking them out. Glug, glug, out of your tank. The most extreme example of a give-away that springs to mind is in a fantastically powerful situation. Take these guys from developed countries who travel, or work, in developing countries. They are, by local standards, extremely rich. Their Clout is massive. They're industrial grade magnets. But, even though they are in demand, they still pay hoes and accept all sorts of unethical behaviour and manipulations. So now hoes are hip that they possess the Balance of Power and won't give them the time of day until they pull their wallets out. Tricks are so retarded and unaccustomed to having the Balance of Power that they just go ahead and bugger things up. There again, if it's my friend he's spoiling, cool.

Possessing the Balance of Power is fundamental. It's no coincidence that I have placed it at the outset of the book. It is of such paramount importance that most of the pages within this book are dedicated to keeping a hoe's tank on "E." Without it, you couldn't even Pimp a "Brewster's Millions" hoe.

We have been sold a dummy. And we did it ourselves, because we got stuck on the idea that power over men was the solution. If we want power and men are powerful, then the trick is to get power over them. Simple. And stupid.
Power & Sex, by Scilla Elworthy

When hoes exploit the Matrix, they are also subject to its inherent drawbacks. They rely on what is basically sex appeal, lust, to attract and "Fort Knox" a man. They have sought security and status instead of true friendship. They are only too aware that their Power slips away with every inch of fat, each fine line, every stretch mark, every grey hair, and if they become a single parent. That each day they draw closer to the menopause. Each year brings with it a new wave of younger, fresher competition. Tick, tick. That's why women spend so much on themselves (or get their trick to) on these creams, beauty treatments, health clubs, fat burning pills and surgery. They are competing with each other for men.

Men, on the other hand, benefit from higher average salaries and positions, have no menopause and rely less on their looks to attract and hold hoes. As they age they become increasingly attractive due to them being able to provide an ever-increasing degree of security and stability, and being more mature minded... Sounds like ideal "daddy" material to me! These factors combined with hers can drive a hoe into a fit over him. Unfortunately, few males are conscious of this gradual turning of the tide. Let alone want to become "rebel" lemmings and go against the grain. The masses would rather have their blue pill, eat their juicy steak and live and die blissfully oblivious, inside the Matrix. Few have the desire and ability to develop and utilise knowledge of how the Matrix is programmed to manoeuvre within it and accomplish their own objectives.

Now let's examine how I obtain and maintain the Balance of Power, and break and bend The Matrix's rules...

The true lover of knowledge naturally strives for truth, and is not content with common opinion, but soars with undimmed and unwearied passion 'till he grasps the essential nature of things.
Plato

A pimp is only as good as his product. And his product is women. You've got to go out there and you've got to get the best ones you can find. And you gotta' work those broads like nobody's ever worked 'em before.
Film: the Mack

A woman will do anything for you if she likes you enough, and you handle her correctly. In order to master a hoe, a Fox must first master himself (Being a Real Man) and then master desire. Iceberg said that a Pimp has an exciting aura of bravado and raw sexiness that would threaten even a nun's morality! Hoe procurement is the most important thing there is to me. Copping is all about provoking hoes to make the first move, how I respond to them, and stabling them. I've got to be walking hoe-bait. The following essays break down the motivational factors that attract hoes to me. There is not a person in the world that there isn't something that will break down their fronting. I don't care who they are. Even that silly hoe who wrote "The Rules."

We all know hoes go for money, bottom line, but they will Choose someone for other, less potent reasons in addition to this. Knowing why a hoe is attracted to me means Power. It enables me to focus on Copping certain classes of hoe and understand how to manage them successfully. The more of each of these virtues I possess, the more hoes will Choose me, the more Environments I'm effective in, and the less they will front.

"Front" can be defined as one's public image. Superficial appearance to others. Looks, car, clothes, jewels, personality, humour, intelligence, who and what one affiliates themselves with, and so on.

Here, I'm going to break it down into my own science. What each Front factor consists of, and follow with an explanation of the circumstances in which each becomes a motivation to a hoe.

• Wealth Front

My Wealth Front hints at my true financial status, my Clout.

Forget the old Sprite adverts. Image is everything! If I look like everyone else, aren't I likely to be like everyone else? Immediately, visually, and from the first time that we speak, it is evident to a hoe that she is not dealing with someone normal or average in any way. I'm a walking question mark.

One thing I can tell you for sure is that, true to stereotype, the five core things that make hoe's minds twitch when they see the light bounce off them are diamonds, fly watches, prestigious homes, prestige cars, fly clothes. Someone who looks like they are exceptional. These same hoes that would otherwise be watching me as much as channel 5 are investigating me like MI5. I could complete a second volume of this book recounting to you tales of hoes transforming like Megatron from poker faced mutes into smiling speak-firsts after catching sight of my wheels. I have literally walked past hoes in the street, then a minute later when they spot me get into my ride, they grease my paint work and poke their noses in the window. Some of them still attempt to front and maintain their hoe code of silence. Don't worry; they notice on the sly. They get real, real curious until they do speak. And when they do, they're opening their brain's trapdoor to me. Like Dracula, I will, and can, only come in if invited.

I dress for first degree murder. I'm dapper each and every day, twenty-four-seven. Shoes as if they're from the box. Car always shimmering like the Cote d'Azure. Silicone on the tyres. I don't get caught with my pants down. I like to look immaculate in every way. I can't have hoes out-dressing a Fox now, can I? All my clothes are my "best" clothes. I like to wear smart but casual, or formal, but not dull, attire. I'm always dressed more formal than my hoes, 'cause, shit, I'm smarter than they are visually too. I put a hoe in her place without a single word. I have a lot of nice clothing, but I don't shop by label. I make sure colours compliment my eyes and skin. I like clothes discretely labelled; it's the look, the quality that counts. I am the brand.

The louder the Front, the more appealing it is to the Low Clout hoes, whereas a more conservative and characteristic Front is more appealing to those with higher Clout, because those who have it flaunt more subtly. Entertainers, bands and singers offer brilliant examples of sensational and diverse Fronts marketed at different strata of society. They offer some serious studying material. Pimp Don "Magic" Juan had his own colour scheme: gold for the honey and green for the money. His suits were tailored in those signature colours, his cars were decked out like that, he even dyed his hair gold - and I mean all his hair!

I let my image express my Clout and personality, and buy what's within my range. This way I will feel comfy and seem casual in it. Daily consistency with what I wear is essential. A Fox isn't afraid to stand out from the crowd, but doesn't appear to be trying to be flashy or showing off. That's not being a Real Man, it's acting. This is a form of insecurity: you can't afford it and it will show. For example, if you wouldn't wear a watch often in case it got scratched, or if you wouldn't drive and park your car most places, you are concerned with its cost in relation to your Clout.

I invest my time and money in myself (well, I'm not going to spend it on anyone else, now am I). The return I receive on it is when it makes more hoes want to invest in me. But I have these indulgences for myself, no one else. Liking them is the only reason I need to buy them. I wouldn't buy a Chupa Chup to pull a hoe, if I wasn't hungry! These items are all replaceable consumer goods, they ain't shit. Hoes are a bonus. I am of the opinion that one's car should be as dapper as one's appearance. Otherwise it is better not to have a banger and use taxis, public transport, and, of course, be taken out. Personal appearance should always be invested in most. Because I could, I got a fly watch years ago. Recently I acquired some ice. I had vowed never to have any carats unless a hoe sponsored them. Otherwise I would have concentrated on the other facets of my appearance until one did. The better I look, the more girls will jock. Would you even give the time of day to some tramp-ass hoodrat who looks like she spends a hell of a lot more on food than she does on clothes? The more affluent I look, the more hoes look, the more confident I'll feel, and this will also manifest itself in my personality. All plusses.

• Emotional & Sexual Front

Although painting a genuine picture of Wealth can be an attraction, a Fox stands out in other aspects too. But the end effect is the same. To draw a hoe into that vortex of desire, flip her into that, "I must have Paradise. No mountain too high. I need to make him mine," hot pussy and purse insanity!

Apart from obvious physical and personal characteristics, it is impossible to isolate Sexual and Emotional Front. They are inextricably intertwined. For example, a smile enhances my Sexual attractiveness, yet also appeals in an Emotional way, since it puts someone at ease, and I appear a nice, settled, comfortable, person. Emotional rapport also invariably leads to Sexual attraction. So I have included them both under the one heading.

When I dress, I do so in front of full-length mirrors. A little narcissm (with a pinch of salt) doesn't do a Fox any harm. There is no such thing as an ugly people, there are just lazy people.

Our inherited, innate physical appearance has relatively little bearing over our Sexual attractiveness. Humour me for a moment and picture in your mind the most physically unattractive, vulgar member of the opposite sex you can imagine! I know it's not pleasant, but go wild on it, make them as absolutely horrible as possible! Do it now, before you continue reading. What really turns you off this person? You will have had to have added the most unattractive physical characteristic in the world: poor hygiene. It's the ultimate turnoff because not only is it disgusting, but it prompts you to subconsciously imagine (or try not to imagine) the vulgar state that their sexual hygiene and health must be in. Therefore my "Law of Opposites" states that I must be extremely disciplined about maintaining a high level of personal hygiene. An immaculate appearance subconsciously conveys this, so does physical fitness. They are the most Powerful Sexual assets in the world.

Cleanliness is close to godliness. I work out regularly and eat properly. Neither is fully effective at shaping one's body without the other. I get my hair cut without fail every few weeks. Manicure weekly, floss frequently, use whitening toothpaste, make use of the cologne I'm given, and get my teeth polished and scaled at least twice a year. Even neaten my eyebrows, which are a little wild. Hairy guys should get their shoulders waxed lose that "werewolf" look! Women should pay attention to any facial and arm hair they have, no matter how slight. Men and women should take particular care concerning the cleanliness or replacement of items that are overlooked by many, such as jewellery, watches, wallets, purses, mobile telephones, keyboards, key rings, bags, and such. Most importantly, I ensure that I get adequate sleep each night. My demeanour, my body language, voice, posture, gestures, facial expressions, they all exude confidence, contentedness, class, success, a certain specialness and sexuality, to provoke women's curiosity. Want to know me more. Desire me, make a move and want to make me theirs. To ensure that they treat me like a king and spoil me like a kid.

I speak with a calm, rhythmic pace. When one talks unhurriedly, one's voice becomes deeper, calmer, sexier, relaxing. It is reassuring and instils confidence. My vocabulary is extensive, I swear less than hoes, I'm knowledgeable, especially concerning life and relationships. I'm an expert communicator: much of which is listening well. It's excellent etiquette to allow others to speak freely, never interrupting. It shows intelligence, control, respect and interest. I often confirm understanding and my interest as the other person talks by nodding, or giving "verbal nods." Besides, if I make up my mind what I'm going to say before the other person finishes, how can I be taking in everything they say? I'm interested in understanding people. When another person is speaking, they become aware that I'm considering all that they say. It shows. This, the fact I pose sentences people have said as questions and I use open and closed questions appropriately allows a person to open up to me more easily without breaking their train of thought.

Wherever I am, in a shop, nightclub, park or restaurant, I don't feel intimidated by my surroundings; I have as much confidence as their proprietor would have. I'm sat as comfortably and relaxed as I would be in my own home, stroll around confidently, feel at ease calling a girl over and talking to her.

I don't walk around looking as if I've been recently diagnosed with a terminal illness. I'm Paradise. The expression on my face reflects that I'm contented, confident, happy and enjoying life. I smile and look happy all the time, but I don't grin at girls. I was already happy before we spoke, not because we spoke. Happiness in itself is attractive. No one wants someone stressful or stressed in their lives. They want to add happiness. People look more attractive when they're smiling. "He has a nice smile. Why is he so happy? He looks fun. His life must be cool. He seems nice. He's always smiley, I wonder why he's never unhappy?"

Because every day of my life is as close to paradise as it can be. Because I always saw green binary code around me, not the Matrix. Because right now, as you're gazing at me, at least eight or nine other women are thinking of me. Because I can see you dazzled, frozen like a rabbit in my headlights. And you're going to bring me some carrots! So, it isn't hard to be a smiling motherfucker, see!

Flirting, in the right context, in the right strength, shows confidence and a sense of fun. One flirt I've adapted from Pimp's and hoe's provocative repertoires, is ensuring my tongue is a little more evident. Now this doesn't appear as conscious, contrived: I'm not talking about looking like a drooling imbecile! Or slowly, overtly, licking my lips like a weirdo. But it can be done in a very subtle, innocuous manner whilst talking. This can range from an almost undetectable glimpse when pronouncing words containing "th" to a more conspicuous slight lip-wetter in-between sentences, as if they're parched.

There are innumerable ways to flirt, often inspired by things that you can observe, and this will be discussed in detail later because flirting is useful not just to attract at the outset, but to interact and enjoy having fun with more overtly. I never take myself too seriously.

On a personal level I'm deep, I'm interesting, I'm fun. I'm a Real Man. I know that experiences and feelings are more valuable than anything material. I'm myself, and I develop myself. Vary and pursue my interests. Borrow books regularly from the library. Travel abroad and domestically. Participate in activities that I have been wanting to do. I might bump into a few hoes at the same time. Better still, I might bump into someone who isn't one. Although a Fox doesn't fall in "luuuurve" with a hoe, he is more in touch with their Emotions than anyone. He has a "direct line" to their feelings, material or Emotional aspirations, hurts, thoughts, soul, strength and fragility. It's just the whole vibe you have. It's intangible, it's difficult to elaborate on. She can really converse openly and deeply with me. It's like I've got that red bat-phone her Emotions dial, but it's a premium rate number. This is the composite result of the character, the integrity, of "Being a Real Man", what is detailed in "Incoming Calls" and the vibe I explain deeper in "The Other Level." This is one of the most powerful things about a Fox. It means that no one can out-talk you. Not many people really understand this.

Someone who doesn't find you attractive has
higher standards than someone who does.
What you can't have you can't resist.
Paradise & Film: Cruel Intentions

Finally, as part of Emotional Front, we come to my "vanity" theory. I believe that people seek approval in the most valid way that they can obtain it. Reassurance of their bare personality and physique, Sexually and Emotionally. Confirmation and nurturing of their own vanity.

Many people spend staggeringly inordinate amounts of money and time on their external vanity. Humans expose their physique, even in public, to a much greater extent than their true persona. We expose our persona to varying degrees, never fully. Validation of personality and physique occurs in two basic forms. In a submissive aspect where someone will do anything for you, tells you that you're the nicest person in the world; no one is more beautiful; they would do anything for you and sympathises with your needs. Your shit doesn't stink to them, which motivates you to crosscheck this sooner or later.

The second way is when someone you perceive to be equal or superior to yourself, to have discerning taste and standards, assess you in a way that is fair, realistic and carries weight. Someone to aspire to. Someone who doesn't go out of their way over you. A person who doesn't find you particularly attractive must have higher standards than someone who does, yes? If the best dressed person in the club compliments you on your appearance a little, your vanity would be affected differently to if a person with chessboard teeth and compost breath approached you and said they liked your aftershave. A guy who tries it on with every female may flatter a woman for a few seconds, but in the back of her mind she knows dogs rub up people's legs when they're desperate.

A Fox should not need to wear out his jaws for a hoe to feel complimented. It shouldn't be much of an effort at all. I'm not sat eating with my mouth open. I speak three languages. Have known women all over the globe. I'm independent and confident. I've worn nothing but satin and RL socks next to my body since seventeen. My saliva isn't stringing to the floor when women strut by. My hair is sharp. I'm not walking around with my head down, slouching. I'm taken world-wide by women, like MasterCard. I'm intelligent, and deeper than a hoe can fathom. I know what a "Grande Cru" Champagne is. My taste is reassuringly expensive like Stella Artois, you know what I'm saying?

I appeal to hoe's egos. I'm unlike anyone else. I'm like a demi-god to them. And a god could never fuck with anyone but a goddess. So girls should be flattered if they even get to speak to me. Three words should always be on a hoe's mind: "Am I worthy?" My friends know I don't compromise on anything. Women feel honoured, privileged to be in my company. I'm only repeating what I hear! Around New Year's Eve they were asking me if they could still see me in the next year. They appreciate that I have allocated a window in my precious time to allow them to take me out. They value the fact that, despite having many "best" female friends, they can still audition. They find just that more complementary than anything most guys could ever say to them, do to them, or do for them. A hoe's vanity is also catered for by my Front when she walks into a room with me, she knows that she's next to the best man there. The best dressed man. The most intelligent man. The sexiest man. More fly than J. R. Hartley. Harder to catch than the Roadrunner. The man a busload of the other hoes in the place are wishing they were with. She feels superior to other people through her association to me. Hoes like to feel that they are in the best, most exclusive company. They also suckers for what others think of them, status. Which brings us to Clout.

Clout

*When you get the money, you get the power. And
when you get the power, you get the women.*
Film: Scarface

Clout is a hoe's sole dominant motivation. Oxygen is a close second.

Whereas Front is image and appearance, Clout is what I am. Actual Wealth, Power, status, position. Ker-ching!

Two guys roar around in sports cars, wearing deep-frozen watches, flashing around obese wallets, plastics named after precious metals. One has debts to the ceiling, credit cards at their limits and is paying the minimum each month. He rents a cramped, one bedroom flat. You get the picture. The other has no mortgage on his house, no finance on his car, savings. Spends two months a year abroad. Both of their Wealth Fronts are equal, but there is a great disparity in their Clout.

Clout is like a smart bomb. It kills off all competition. It's far more important than any Front. Hoes like someone fit, good looking, deep, funny, but it helps if you are financially stable. Hoes jock large Clout, full stop. Irrelevant of six-packs, stand-up comic skills, or if you can make them pass out in bed. A hoe will always "upgrade" to someone with superior Clout or with huge Potential. She may want to indulge her Sexual and Emotional sides, but they are comparatively insignificant, non-essentials.

Front gets, Clout keeps.
The Kidd

Do you see male actors, politicians, sport celebrities, musicians, royalty, company directors and executives stuck for dates, wives or mistresses? Cast your eyes over the last generation of actors and actresses. How many of each sex have undergone some kind of cosmetic surgery as they reach old age? How many divorcees from celebrities revert back to their unknown maiden names?

Some people fortunately have inherent Clout. Prince William. Do you think if William was born a nobody and sold the Big Issue on a corner that women would batter an eyelid? Don't tell me if you made a hit record, or starred in the latest blockbuster, "long lost" friends wouldn't suddenly jam your phone line. That those women who treated you as the invisible man, who never had time to yap wouldn't instantaneously develop eyesight and conversational skills. That you wouldn't receive fan mail from people who didn't even know you. When a hoe asks me what I do, what I drive, what university I went to, or if I live with my parents, she's not making conversation. The answer will determine whether she is "cool" with me, or if she goes into heat, goes all out to pull me and tie me down like Gulliver.

[Hoes] are like monkeys. They won't let go of
one branch until they have hold of another.
Film: Mission Impossible 2

To conclude my description of Front and Clout, let's look at how I use this knowledge practically. The best way to determine motivation is to look at what a hoe does and doesn't have in her life. Not at how she's interacting with me.

For instance, I know that if a hoe with higher Clout than I Chooses me, her primary motive with me has to be Emotional, Sexual, or both. Unless she sees mad Potential in me.

Hoes with less Clout than I will get excited over an ostentatious, lavish Front. They're going to be dazzled by my lifestyle, places I travel to, things I've done, names, my Wealth Front and Clout. However people with higher Clout aren't too concerned about how much ice I'm wearing in the same way. They've already got the T-shirt. They're looking at me from a more Sexual and Emotional viewpoint, see. They may like the ice, the watch aesthetically and find me attractive in my clothes. But they're thinking of me in the emperor's new clothes. They want to just do it like Nike. Or they're on an Emotional trip, they've got that feeling inside like Lexus. This doesn't change the fact that Clout is a hoe's primary motivation.

A classic example of this would be someone whose career position is senior to mine, who normally wouldn't even consider someone below her level. Or perhaps she is attached to someone with Clout. She has put herself in those golden handcuffs. Clout is the only key that will unlock them. It's a sad reality that some hoes will have simply got the man with the largest Clout they could find to take them down the isle. He could be a twenty stone ogre, on his deathbed, with the personality of a traffic warden. She's still going to be signing those cheques and card slips "Mrs Ogre." Any Emotional or Sexual virtues he happens to possess are merely a bonus to her. Other hoes will slightly downgrade on Clout in order to get someone more fun or handsome. But as long as they place Clout in the equation, they're hoeing.

In some cases her trick may be friends with her, but they're not Sexually compatible (this will actually undermine their platonic friendship anyway). Or they may hit it off in bed, but Emotion is missing (the absence of Emotion will undermine Sexual gratification, creating another void in her life). Should they hit all three Front, plus Clout, then of course, she will not going to be looking around in a hurry. Unless a man has double the Clout of her husband. Welcome to the rat-race.

So a hoe normally creates these voids in her life by her very own nature, whilst paper-chasing. They often try to compensate for the Emotional gap by attempting to form closer friendships with their friends, pets, relations, parents, or focusing over-intensely on children. All are in danger of, and many do, compensate for marrying for money by having an affair with someone possessing the missing qualities. They're missing good Emotions, Emotional Sex, Sexual attraction and mind-blowing Sex. One is never far behind the other.

Sometimes a cheating hoe can get confused. And they will confuse their lover. They notice how great their life now seems and assume that the reason must be the affair. So they convince themselves and their lover that they should become a couple. They forget that the first box (Clout) was already ticked by marrying. And so around in a circle they might eventually go, by leaving Clout for Emotional and Sexual reasons, only to discover they are now missing their priority: Clout. And the hunt for Clout begins again.

I do not advise having affairs. You will put yourself at risk and your property at risk.

Some attached men and women try to hide their status, but they will invariably fail due to the many giveaways and the way a Fox operates, which is laid out later. So it is not difficult to avoid married, or cheating people.

Furthermore, it will demean you if you participate in any kind of sneaking around and hiding. That is not being a Fox: that is taking on work, taking on problems. If someone says that they are going to get divorced, or finish a relationship, let them go do it. If they do, then they can come back, and that is when you can consider a relationship of any sort: either exclusive, or non-exclusive, where you are both single and dating.

This clear Front analysis took me a time to suss as I observed all that went on around me. I would think to myself, "One day I'll figure out why things transpire as they do. There have to be logical Laws by which these things are governed. When I understand what forces are at work here, I'll be more powerful than the rear end of a space shuttle.

The key is: if a hoe has to choose between leaving Clout for anything else, she will not go. But she's going to be around me forever if she is in the frame of mind where she understands she doesn't need to pick between Clout and Emotion and Sex. For example, when you are single, you can date who you want, when you want. Mix and match. Or if your family takes care of your financial needs you can be free to look for the other two desires in a relationship. Or perhaps your career takes care of your precious Clout needs, at least for the moment. I may need to Package this to her. All she needs to do is add positive things to her life. To the ones she already has.

I'm not interested in trying to satisfy a hoe's Clout (I am interested in helping her to improve her own, in an advisory aspect detailed later.) As long as she doesn't feel like she's jeopardising her Clout, a hoe is wide open to what she doesn't have. So it isn't rocket science to figure how we're a combination. I tell them I'll be the best friend they ever had, if they treat me right, but I can never be anyone's boyfriend. I tell hoes "As long as you're good to me, all you ever need worry about is where to go." They say it's the sweetest thing that didn't come in a wrapper. As you now see, one doesn't need platinum cards to attract wealthy hoes. You don't necessarily have to go to New Bond Street, have more rocks than Whitby Bay, or a five-figure car, just as long as you have your Emotional and Sex Front. It could be loud n' proud, rugged, kind of cultural, spiritual, business-like, or conservative understated elegance.

One doesn't need to be physically fit to attract low Clout hoes. I want to make the point that anyone can be a Fox, irrelevant of them being fat, thin, shy, outgoing, rich, poor, or having a scarred face. But if you're not a Real Man, interesting, happy, or immaculate, you're in trouble. Whatever a Fox's status, personality, or weight, he or she can apply logic to their own virtues and utilise them in the most suitable Environments, on the most eligible hoes. Obviously the more Front one has, the more effective scope and versatility.

A poor but well-defined, sexy, friendly and deep gas station attendant, fitness instructor, or gardener in an affluent area of town is in a good position to be Chosen by a high Clout hoe. She is likely to see him when solo, under relatively informal circumstances, will already be interacting with him, and will see him repeatedly, which is important to manifest desire for him. If I want a budget hoe, I can cruise through my local council estate with the windows down and hey presto... I hear the young hoes, "Hey! I like your car. Take me for a ride?"

I was never the best looking, nor the best. Among my contemporaries there were fabulously beautiful people. And I had to have an edge. My edge was always class.
Iceberg Slim

Environment

I'm only as good as my competitor is bad.
Stephen R Covey

If I can be seen, I can be Chosen. If I can be Chosen, I can be a Fox.

I don't hermit around at home all week. I get some exposure. The more women who see me, the more will be able to Choose me. My friends and I often prefer to socialise out rather than visit each other's houses. This means we look more interesting, relaxed and content when in clubs and bars, or anywhere, because we're busy talking and not there to pull with nothing to do.

It's sensible to be an irregular rather than a regular at nightspots and such places. Less than fortnightly is sufficient to do this. This has a triple benefit. I'm catching a hoe's eye repeatedly, yet reducing fronting by not constantly being there. I also cover more territory, see more places, more places see me. At clubs, the pool, the beach, and in the street, my Sexual and Wealth Fronts will draw the hoes. At work, social occasions, classes, on the net and in most sports - informal interactive Environments - my Emotional Front has more opportunity to attract.

Preferred and most successful Copping Environments vary from Fox to Fox, place to place. Every gentleman of leisure has their own favourites that their individual Front works best for them in. For some reason, I have always had women speak to me in supermarkets. Because my wheels are tight, I get blatant signals in car parks, or in a late night eatery I have a habit of frequenting just after the pubs close. I pull my time machine up nearly in front of the door. That's like pick n' choose time for me! And I don't have to start a conversation. Hoes in bars and pubs still make themselves known, but front more. Especially in groups of three or over (applicable to any Environment). Hoes love an audience to act in front of. They have their companions on their mind, and often in their ear too.

Plus they may be intoxicated, which is useless. My particular least effective Environment is in clubs. It's usually friends of friends who make moves on me in them. People are usually going out to Front when they hit the club on a Friday night. From how they dress to how they act. Networking is a valuable Copping tool to a Fox, because Emotional and Sexual Copps are facilitated through informal contact. A male or female I'm just cool with, a relative, even parents, may unwittingly introduce me to my next hoe. Dinner parties and barbecues are informal, yet there are always new faces. Foxes can even help each other by getting their hoes to refer their friends to other Foxes. Now that's beautiful! The standards that Front and Clout are measured by in each location and situation are set by the following factors that The Kidd devised. These are useful to bear in mind when planning to go to a club, mall, supermarket, park, beach, or to grab a snack. Foxes never adapt to their hoes or Environment like players do. Our principles are unwaivable. If the conditions aren't favourable, I migrate to greener pastures.

• **Other's Front & Clout**

I have a sports car, designer clothes, a decent watch, reasonable career, immaculate appearance. When I'm rolling through small towns and average areas, girls holler. If I pull up outside an average club, my machine is the best in the parking lot. Heads swivel. When I go inside, I'm dressed dapper, I stand out like a reggae band at a Klan rally. I'm at the top of the food chain. Hoes will wonder what I do and if I'm too out of their league to step to. Hoes will be itching to cut into me. Others in the club around me haven't got that level of Front or Clout. Whereas driving in Kensington or pulling up to a premium club in the capital city, I'm next to Jags, Mercedes, Lexus, Porches, Martins, Bentleys, BMWs and Ferraris. And when I'm inside, I'll probably look so-so. I might look worth robbing, but the person standing next to me might have more ice than fast food restaurant drinks on him. They may have a nation-wide reputation and recognition due to their Clout. His bank book might look like a phone directory. I'm a small fish, surrounded by big-timers, executives, celebrities. Who's going to look? It's all about who else is around. They set the precedent for my Front and Clout. I'm only as good as my competitor is bad.

• Demographics

We're talking supply and demand. The ratio of men to women is an important factor.

If the area I am in has three men to every woman, the climate encourages heavy tricking. Women will have choice. Men will be making the moves. All hoes will be seen to be mint because there just aren't that many of them. The hoes will be real choosy, as they're getting offers left right and centre.

I really want to go for an Environment where females outnumber males. Men will be at a premium. Ever been in that situation? The hoes will be competing for me, no effort on my part. Most men don't take real advantage of such an opportunity.

Men are typically in short supply at dance, yoga, and massage and cookery classes. At equestrian activities and events. Women are normally in shorter supply at golf clubs, car clubs, martial art classes and mixed gyms. It's not possible to make a long or definitive list of ideal Environments: a club may be full of females on one night because two celebrations coincide, but the next week be full of males. A French evening class may be full of females in your town, but full of males in mine. So one must simply get out there and be aware of the demographics wherever they are. You may be able to build a castle in a swamp, but why, when you can build on rock?

Choosing

A hoe can either Choose me or loose me.
Paradise

Take a college student; we'll call him Simon. He's infatuated with a classmate. He can't remove his eyeballs from her when she's around. He's projecting all his desires onto her personality, as he doesn't really know her. He's certifiably crazy about her. Because he is eager to impress, Simon jumps to "lend" Claire some money when she asks him. He often buys lunch for her in the refectory. Pretends to be interested in subjects that she is. Tries to like the same music as her. Persuades his friends to go out with him to a club that Claire frequents. Offers her lifts, as she doesn't drive. Gives her a driving lesson. Allows her to smoke in his car. Claire tells Simon that he's nice and flirts with him at the time, when he does something kind for her, but things never progress beyond a kiss.

One day, as graduation nears, Simon finally makes a move and expresses his true feelings to Claire. Classic behaviour: fronting always reduces at such times. Her reaction is at best sickly sweet, "That's really nice. I'm flattered, but sorry no. Let's just be friends, hey." Or worst, well suffice to say that she pulls a face like she tasted some Marmite and tells him to do something physically impossible.

He wasted months gathering the confidence to ask her out. Because he was focused on her, he missed several real prospects that were giving him Evidence whilst he was in his warp. He then consumed more of his time and money as he set about trying to impress her, hoping that his artificial Behaviour would make her become attracted to him. He tried to become the sort of person that he presumed Claire wanted. Forfeiting his own life, and development as a man.

By adhering to a simple principle, he could have avoided that, and any kind of distantly related situation.

There is simply no logic in Choosing someone who is

not Choosing me. First a girl has to "Choose" me, be attracted to me, before I can consider her at all.

I will describe how I deduce this subsequently. It is the key to minimising time and energy wasted. It's my filter. It means no longer is pulling based on irrelevant assumptions, a guessing game or game of chance... "If I speak to ten women, at least one will be down. Once a model went for me, and she's not as fit, so she should like me. She says she is married. Someone said she has a boyfriend. She's wearing a ring so she's not single. She says she doesn't like me. I'm too old for her. I'm too young for her. She talked to my friend more than me, so she likes them." Or, "I had better let her know I like her otherwise nothing will ever happen."

Because I can smell attraction, I'm exclusively selecting from and dealing with girls that are already consciously or subconsciously jocking me. I know that they're interested without any lame talking to them or asking around.

The masses plugged into the Matrix are seriously out of touch with this principle. A woman is not going anywhere unless she Chooses to. She's either in that frame of mind or not. Therefore I don't believe that any third party can "break up" a relationship. They can intend to, but they need an accomplice. See, there is no such thing as someone "stealing" someone else's woman - unless they are literally kidnapping them against their will!

I'm happy for anyone who finds their relationship fulfilling. But women and men aren't property.

This kind of ignorance used to result in far out shit such as pistols at dawn! Nowadays people still stupidly fight for one another's attention, be it physically, sexually, beauty-wise, personality-wise or with money. Now this is what I love my hoes to do with me. But I'm outside the Matrix. I could never go out of my way over a hoe. I'm true to myself. A hoe can either Choose me or loose me.

Where power is, love is not.
C J Jung

Ignoring the Choosing principle pumps up the sought person's ego and compromises mutual respect. Once someone takes the step of attempting to make another Choose them more than they actually do, the process of exchanging false Behaviour in the hope of gaining affection, sex, money, whatever, begins. The seeker is being deceptive, therefore cannot fully respect the sought. The sought knows, or eventually realises this. The sought may take advantage of this fact and manipulate the seeker to get what they want too. Both parties have usually been doing that from day one. When one party is trying to realise their needs by compromising mutual respect there are only two things the other should do. Terminate the relationship and find a true friend - good luck! Or else decide that the exchange rate between what they want and what they will have to compromise in order to get it is acceptable. Then continue in order to obtain what they want from each other.

You will note that I will occasionally refer to subconscious attraction. By this I mean that a woman can start considering Choosing me and not even be consciously aware of it. It can take time before what's manifesting in her subconscious becomes a conscious thought that she is aware of. It can take a lot of pressure, a lot of question marks and desires mounting before the dam between the rear and front of her brain busts.

Only peasants seek security in the passions of the heart.
Trick Baby, by Iceberg Slim

Now on to one of my favourite Matrix, "Simon Says" traditions. Marriage. If people were honest, they wouldn't promise to be each other's until death parts them.

In reality, if in two days or ten years they are no longer Choosing each other, they would be wasting one another's life if they did not split. Yes, I agree that people can feel like they could spend forever with each other, and can do so. Except it's conditional on them continuing to get along. Continuing to make an effort. Change is as certain as death and taxes. Everyone changes over time. Why did they get together and feel like that in the first place? You don't decide you like someone and it's, "they lived happily ever after." Liking someone isn't a decision that you can resign yourself to. It's an opinion that is formulated each hour, every day, every week, every year.

People often use the tradition of a marriage ceremony as a means to try and fool themselves around this Law of Reality, and to obtain a "secure future" with another. Often meaning a secure financial future. If people are deterred from ending relationships by fear, legalities, finances, children or other people's opinion, then yes, it will help keep them under the same roof. The truth is the biggest, purest compliment you can have is for someone who is entirely free to go any second, actually Choosing to be with you every moment that they spend in your company. This is how my women and I are. My relationships have always been based on positive forces. Desire, honesty, respect, happiness, not fear.

Evidence

As a mack you have to listen with your eyes.
K-Flex

Proper use of observation allows me to distinguish between a prospect and a dead horse with ease. With time and practice, these skills have become second nature to me. I suss people out real quick. I see straight through any bullshit and fronting. It's like I'm that guy in "What Women Want." No kidding. This coupled with my understanding of human nature, psychology and Behaviour means, even more Powerfully, I always know far more about a woman than she tells me. I can prophesise her future actions and reactions.

Observation adds logic, knowledge and therefore confidence to my game. I know who's Choosing me, which means I know who I can Choose from. I'm not dependent on them to confirm their attraction to me. I don't need to ask around. I never look desperate. It also helps me to be patient. Knowledge is Power alright.

Wherever I am, whatever I'm doing, I'm prepared to Copp. Being a Fox isn't a part time job. It's a mindset. I don't specifically go out to Copp. Although I take Environmental factors into account - I want the best odds - I do what I want to do. If I want to learn French, why attend an evening class with five men in it when there is one with one male and six females in it?

Evidence will arise eventually. I could be in a club, restaurant, park, shooting range, street, class, church event, bar, charity barbecue, library, pool, dentist's waiting room, shopping centre, petrol station, or at the beach. I may be talking to her to order a meal or we may have never exchanged words, it doesn't matter. There are basic Behavioural patterns that I class as "Evidence."

If a hoe is attracted to me, she won't be able to help placing herself in my proximity, or taking a position from which she can gander at me. A girl leans up to the bar near me when most of the bar is free. She walks past me to put something into the bin when there is one closer to her. Asks me for a light when I'm not the nearest person to her. Stands facing my direction whenever using the photocopier. Faces me when chatting to people in my vicinity. Turns around the longest way. Turns her head. That kind of thing. Of course, it can translate into a thousand situations.

Hoes don't get my attention. They seek it. I allow them to appreciate me without the interruption of confrontation. Reciprocation, interaction, is not imperative in order to be desired and obsessed over. Entertainers are some of the most fantasised about people in the world. I stroll and drive sloooow, to allow the hoes to get an eyeful. Giving them time to enjoy the view, make a move, and me the time to collect Evidence. But I'm not wandering around, driving or sat looking over my shoulder like some trick, openly scanning the place. I'm not watching tennis. I look where I'm facing. I would walk past Medusa as if she were invisible. I never lower my eyes submissively, I look beyond the hoe. I act like I have blinkers on, like I have tunnel vision. But I am aware of my surroundings; I might catch a head turning in my peripheral vision. If a hoe is Choosing me in a slower Environment such as a club or at work, she will eventually manoeuvre herself into my field of vision. If I can see her, she can see me. A glance, a stare that lasts that bit longer. She looks once, twice, I pay no mind. She looks five, six times, I take note. The quieter the surroundings, the stronger the Evidence.

The first thing you want to do is set up a base of operations. Sit yourself down somewhere and remain stationary. Fight the temptation to explore your surroundings. That makes you look hungry. Trust me, if a bitch likes what she sees, she will put herself in your perimeter. Just make sure you are sitting somewhere highly visible. Be the first one in the club to get a good seat if you have to. What you want to keep an eye out for is what I call a perimeter breach.
The Kidd

There is close range Evidence too. Women have less white in their eyes and better peripheral sight, their eyes being wider apart. So it's easier to notice hoes looking when they're near. The positive side to this is that I don't need to be in a hoe's face for her to spot me.

She exclaims things aloud to herself when near me. She initiates conversations, smiles at me, or says hi first. Because I won't be! In a supermarket she might remark about something I have picked off the shelf. Stutters if put under any pressure. Asks me my name. Probes my Clout. Opens up a lot about herself. Goes all quiet, but not "bored" quiet. Plays with her hair, necklace, ring, pen, or fidgets with her mobile, or any objects incessantly when in my presence. Messes with her hair like she has fleas. When she's looking at me or we're chatting, her neck artery swells, her cheeks or lips bloom if not wearing makeup, eyes appear wider open, or her pupils saucer under daylight conditions. Goes out of her way to do something for me. Tactileness. Places her elbow next to mine, sits close. Touches my arm. Molests my hand when she puts change into it. Rests her foot on my stool leg. Any invasion of my personal space. I don't take that friendly nudge as nothing. It gets added to the Evidence.

There may be other reasons behind her Behaviour. She may be interested in the person next to me. A waitress might flirt to obtain a tip. She may prefer to sit where she is. There may be a source of wind, heat or cold that she is moving to or away from. Over time, I can gather Evidence, strengthen Evidence and build my case. I may sit somewhere else for a change and observe if she reacts. Sit at a different table in the restaurant I frequent regularly and see if she still serves me. Position myself so that her view of me is obscured and watch if she leans back or cranes her neck. Observe and compare how she interacts with other people. Does she go around beaming at everyone? Obviously I can see if they're the kind of person who flirts and is generally physical or not. If so, the value of that particular nature of Evidence depreciates accordingly.

The value of Evidence is also determined by the length of our contact and if we are likely to meet again. This afternoon a woman approached me in a car park, not in my hometown, asking if I wanted her ticket that still had an hour left on it. In that surprise situation I had to quickly assess any possible Evidence. I only required the slightest, as my contact with her would have been mere seconds.

Did she choose to approach me instead of somebody else nearer to her? Couldn't she see the ticket displayed in my window next to her? Did she say anything else less formal? In this instance, her face read like a child's first book, she couldn't conceal her excitement as she smiled and her wide blinking eyes kept catching mine like I had tractor beams.

Speech was given to man to disguise his thoughts.
Charles Maurice de Telleyrand

People would rather have us listen to what they're saying than trust our observations of facts, of what they are actually doing. Wedding rings (some are false), talk of (real or imaginary) boyfriends, husbands, someone they're after, being in love, never being unfaithful, or wanting to be just friends are not indicative of a hoe's mindset. What people say is simply what they want you to hear. Hoes spend most of their waking hours fronting reeeeal good. Most men wouldn't believe what's going on in these nonchalant women's minds. I'm sure hoes think they'll drop dead if they totally cease fronting, like sharks do if they stop swimming. I watch actions. When a woman walks past me, smiles and purrs, "Hi." she's not saying it to exercise her jaw muscles. It does sound presumptuous to assume that, because a member of the opposite sex speaks to me first, or feels up my hand when handing me coins, she's Choosing me, but it usually is the case. It's highly incriminating Evidence. Believe me. Do you really think she walked around the corner and said hi to the next person that she passed? This is tried and tested. I have always found I'm correct, sometimes only minutes or hours, sometimes days or months after, when the hoe stops fronting and makes her move.

The Law of Reciprocation

*A good boss always gives them just enough to keep
'em coming, but not enough to stop them coming.*
Paradise's Grandfather

The Law of Reciprocation states that I should Reciprocate
as little as possible up to a maximum of twenty five
percent in respect of hoe's physical and verbal Behaviour
if they will see me repeatedly. Up to a maximum of fifty
percent if they aren't likely to see me again.

The reasons for the Law are numerous. To entice a
woman and heighten her desire. To ensure and
encourage that she pursues me. To eliminate time
wasters who are just seeking a little ego boost. To add
mystique. To maintain the Balance of Power.

When a mint girl with more features than my car walks
down the street or enters the room, all the tricks are
openly leering at her curves and elbowing their friends.
All the other women in the vicinity notice this too. She
sees it all every day. She knows they are just going off
her looks. She knows what they want. How can you
really like someone until you know them? I haven't even
glanced at her.

Me, my approach is, well, she looks okay, that's only
one thing, I don't know her. To me a small, nevertheless
important part of attraction is physical appearance. The
greater part has always been how a person is, what
they're like on a personal level. Now I'm not detracting
from physical beauty at all. What I'm saying is that if a
woman is unclean, dumb, uncaring, dishonest, lacks
initiative, generosity, is closed with me, disrespectful, or
I dislike her personality, it turns me off her like I would
be if she had slid down their skirt and pulled out a dick!

Ideally someone would have virtues in both areas.
Fortunately I have naturally always been like this. Very
selective and choosy. Over the years it's given me
experiences that I have analysed and developed many of
my hypothesis from.

57

I think the guys thinking with their dicks are shallow. They compromise everything for looks. True Intimacy, the best sex, is not exclusively physical. They're desperate for sex. She'd have to prove herself before she qualified with me. This makes me stand out to her. I don't even waste my time looking, thinking about her, greeting or chatting to her until it's in line with Reciprocation. Simply the fact she's been around me for an hour and she's not seen me glimpse at her starts to twist her brain, as she's the shit, isn't she? All women crave attention to feed their vanity. I've not tried even talking to her when she's chatting to people within my group. Why am I not up her ass like everyone? She knows that simply looking pretty doesn't get her anywhere with me. She's aware everyone wants to jump on her because of her looks. It's meaningless because it is a default, standard status. Perhaps she subconsciously seeks reassurance of her personality. If, somewhere in the back of her brain she's starting to Choose me, she will get curious.

I should be seen, not heard, and only speak when spoken to.
Paradise

Once a girl steps and starts interacting with me in any conscious way, such as talking, smiling, direct eye contact, or subconscious ways such as glancing, facing me and coming near me, Reciprocation commences. Until then, I don't do anything except get on with my life.

The Law of Reciprocation applies universally all the time I'm dealing with a hoe. She initiates all forms of contact, except when I'm Rewarding Behaviour. I conclude all forms of contact. I let her say hi first. I let her speak to me first, I conclude all conversations. She talks about going out. She brings up the subject of sex. I Reciprocate according to how often we see each other. The more often, the less. If a hoe positions herself so that I'm in her field of vision, I ensure that I'm not facing completely away from her. If a hoe is glancing, the correct way to Reciprocate is first she looks, and whilst she is, I look. Then I always look away before she does. At work, or in any interactive situations, I conduct myself pleasantly with female colleagues and acquaintances on a formal level. I'm friendly and let them develop personal conversation if they feel inclined. There is a woman in my company that ganders and smiles in my direction daily, as she does with several guys. She's on a little ego-boosting mission. I only allow her a momentary glance from me once a week. It's all about psychology and motivation, which is covered later on. It's all about not too little, not too much!

I use higher Reciprocation, up to fifty percent, for situations where contact is brief and we are unlikely to meet again. In a car park or mall, a hoe may only be able to look at me four times before one of us leaves. I look back twice. For every ten times a hoe in a supermarket eyes me, I glance, smile back four or five.

Say there's a woman who calls, "Hello!" every time she sees me. We bump into each other every week. I say hi back. Nothing else. Sometimes she might follow it with a, "How are you?" and I answer. The conversation then dies and I split unless she adds to it. Every three or four times she asks me how I am, I'll Reciprocate, ask her back. When I reply, I don't tell her my life story, but I give her something that she can expand on, ask me about, if she wants to. I don't flippantly mumble, "I'm okay." I tell her, "Actually things are really hectic, but I'm really good." Or, "I had a fabulous /unusual/strange/relaxing weekend, thank you." Then if she wants to, it isn't hard for her to cut into me by getting curious. Of course as soon as she does, I hit her with the "Contract." "Well a friend took me to a really nice place on Friday night." Or, "I went away for the weekend." See how I'm giving her more questions with each answer than she can ask? A good answer leads to many more questions. Bad conversation leads to none. See how I'm not talking more than she does? Also she's asking three quarters of the questions. This intriguing, vague, sought after style applies to all methods of communication.

I start building up a picture of inside her head as we chat. I'm friendly. I have fun, have a laugh. I note what information she's obtaining from me. She'll be sizing me up during this and our next few chats. This will also give me insight into her mind. It's the ideal opportunity to size her up too. As she's doing this I answer her and Reciprocate by mirroring some questions, especially if they're deep. Add the odd one of my own. I'm still deciding if she qualifies, if I want her. It's cool if she gets the impression I'm assessing her personal qualities, and Clout, if she has less than I. She should.

There are exceptions to the Law of Reciprocation. Spending money, flattery - other than Emotional, and verbal and physical flirting, which also needs to be checked hard. If a hoe touches me, even slightly, or comes into my "comfort zone" I react like she's stuck my finger in a mains socket!

I never let a hoe catch me checking out anything but her eyes. Not her body or her clothes. I would only look at her torso if she was mine and we were getting intimate. I never ever pay attention to her Clout, car, ice, house or anything of hers, even if she is checking mine. That would be a bad signal. I look directly into her windows when we're exchanging glances or linguistics.

The Contract

I wasn't asking, I was telling!
Paradise

The instant that a hoe and I begin to exchange words informally, no matter the circumstances, there are several points I lay down during the conversation. This information is shared during our first and second informal contact. Only in exceptional circumstances do some spill over into later conversations, such as there being insufficient time or opportunity. But I allow her to create the opportunity. I'll show you how.

The "Contract" can be set out in a couple of sentences. It's simplicity itself to drop it when engaged in conversation. It's relevant to many topics that are typically discussed "Do you come here often?" "What's your itinerary for the forthcoming week?" "What have you been up to lately?" "Any plans for the weekend?" "Are you single?" "How are you?" all present the opportunity to include it in my response.

At worst, questions can be encouraged by Engineering the conversation a little. I load a question into my response to something she says. This can also be used indefinitely to create and maintain intrigue. I showcased this in The Law of Reciprocation chapter. Here are a few additional examples.

"Why do you have to go so soon?" "You're tanned, been on holiday?" "I like your shirt."

I reply, "I have to be up early because I'm going away." "Thanks, I was given some tan sessions as a present." "This? It was a really thoughtful gift actually, because I'm very hard to buy for. I'm so choosy." Now she's got plenty of opportunity to converse.

Alternatively I can ask her what she has done lately. She is bound to return the question. Even supposing that she doesn't, I can now go ahead and advise her of how busy I am anyway.

"I went to a restaurant I've never been to before." Or, "I went out to dinner with a friend." Or, "I went on a date."

If using the word "friend" I eventually identify my friend as female by including a "she," or their name, somewhere. Women then often enquire about the friend or this new date and if the feminine reference wasn't first included, now it can be referred to. "She's one of my best friends/just a date/someone who just asked me out/a good friend." Or ask about the meal. "I had fish, she had chicken." Or the place. "I don't know where it is, I could ask her, I suppose." Next come the girlfriend questions. I reply no. If asked why, I reply that I like my friend because of certain essential qualities, she is thoughtful, fun, considerate, has good taste, and so on. But I'm only dating at the moment, or just want to be friends.

I am, in essence, smoothly laying out the Contract. Things she must accept in order that she can deal with me. It's her choice, but I'm not asking directly. I'm just sharing information with her about me. Showing her how to get somewhere with me. No one is forcing her to talk to me again or call me. They always do though. They're already Choosing me strongly.

I want to stress that I never brag, over-emphasise things, enquire what she is looking for, or about her marital status. Those are not my problems. I'm not asking, I'm telling! It's all about me, myself and I.

The main points of my Contract that I like to set out are listed below. I don't necessarily come out with the points as I've written them, unless she's Choosing me hard and I have absolute Power. Then I can lay them down like a General or like Ginger does with Sam Rostine in "Casino." I'll adapt them to our conversation. The reasons behind this information will become apparent in due course.

- **Perhaps we could be friends.**

She's being assessed as well as having a fun, friendly conversation, and this fact is not hidden. She's auditioning, she hasn't got the role. If a girl is pushy, I emphasise that I need to know her further to ascertain this. In my mind my standard is: I can't even consider anything like dates until it's justified by knowing her a little and her giving me reasons to like her, besides physical ones.

When a woman responds to me at any time by inferring I am after sex or a girlfriend, she's just sparring, trying to figure me, and her position, out. I let her know she isn't with the program. I hardly even know her. I'm maybe after a good friend. But that's in her hands. Anything else is futuristic optimism on her part.

• I am not looking for a girlfriend.

Because this can be misinterpreted as promiscuity or shirking responsibility, I might elaborate, but minimally. I honestly state my reasons. I'm happy in my life at the moment. Most of my best friends are female in fact. Friendship is most important to me. After all, friendship is the basis of any good relationship. And it takes a long time to thoroughly get to know someone.

I've experienced relationships with women all over the world. I've learnt a lot about myself and also about what I want. I'm realistic. I don't think I would find a girlfriend even if I looked, because I never compromise on the things in my life. I wouldn't accept second best. I think the more attributes you demand, the less likely you are to find a person with them all. I'm selective enough about my friends.

It's like people can be categorised into the shape of a pyramid. At the bottom, its widest point, are the majority of people. Those whom you can get on with at work, talk to superficially, be generally pleasant with, but you have little else in common. The next level up, there will be the people who you can have a laugh with, or who make interesting conversation. Rise further up, and you have an even narrower level consisting of individuals who possess all those previous qualities combined. The following level, even fewer people who also respect you, who are honest with you. If they're attractive to you too, they have initiative, intelligence and are caring, they'll go to the next level. As you ascend further and further towards the apex, the fewer people, if any, who possess all the qualities to be yours.

• I date. I get asked out. I don't ask women out or take them on dates.

I mention I was asked out, taken out, I have friends who occasionally Invite me on dates with them, or take me places, during our conversation.

If she asks why, I explain that I find it more flattering to be asked out. I'm easygoing. I don't take for granted that people wish to be in my company, so I allow them to come to me. I'm not comfortable with going out with someone unless they feel comfortable enough with me to ask me. I allow someone to decide if they wish to socialise with me at their own natural pace.

I'm too busy to plan outings. Plus, if I'm not worth taking out, then they weren't the right person anyway, we both should be spending time with someone else. I like to know someone really wants to see me. I like a woman to be up-front, down to earth, mature, open, caring and have initiative. Those are the most appealing qualities she could have. They are essential.

• My time is at a premium.

I lead a very busy, varied, active life. Socially, leisure and business wise. This comes across easily in conversation and is backed up by my actions. When women ask me what my interests are, I tell them all of them. They usually ask me where I find the time. If asked what I've done recently, my schedule will speak for itself. I often remark that things are hectic and I need a time here and there just to chill. This point is enforced in some ways that I will describe later.

Potential

He who thinks in terms of catching
mice will never catch lions.
Andrew Stonewall Jackson

Time is money. The last thing I want to do is waste it on a lame that will never clear the first jump, when there are thoroughbreds out there. I want to enjoy my time with someone worthwhile.

It's important to be able to swiftly rate a hoe's Potential value to me in order to decide initially if she qualifies with me.

Later, Potential will allow me manage my own expectations to reflect reality, and assess how much she's really doing for me compared to what she could be. I don't want to expect, or ask, for things that are hard or impossible to do. Neither do I want to be impressed by something that, to her, is very little effort. This will allow me to Reward her Behaviour appropriately.

Fox principle is to accept, conditionally of course, all hoes with good Potential that Choose me, if I'm not in an exclusive relationship. But if my time is full already, she must be better Potential than my worst relationship and meet whatever other standards I have. A full stable isn't definable in terms of numbers. It depends how much time one wishes to spare. So if her Potential is low and I have my life full of Top Performers with huge Potential, I pass and make better use of my time.

All the time a hoe is checking my Potential out, I'm assessing her Potential too. We're doing the same thing! Noticing watches, occupation, clothes, vehicles, children attending a private school, signs of good or bad financial management, where she's been on vacation, family, and where she lives. I can do this quite quickly and blatantly with hoes that have less Clout than I. They facilitate this process when they ask me those, "What do you do?" questions. It is perfectly natural to mirror them.

Hoes whose Clout higher than mine are assessed patiently, prudently and discretely. I don't care about specifics, just a general idea. There's no rush. I Wait for them to voluntarily indicate their Clout. It is inappropriate to try to be direct. I think hoes and Foxes divide other people they meet into five rough categories, according to their Potential, which I will now explain.

• Low Clout

I avoid them like the plague. It's sensible to have a few on the side, to maintain a great sex life, since I don't act like a nympho with the rest of the stable. Dealing with one of these for any other reason would just consume my valuable time, which could be spent with people with more Potential.

A grade A student in the same circumstances is worth a look. Or a minta. It's a travesty that she should be signing on, or leaning behind a counter asking me if I would like to super-size my meal. A minta can always increase her status. They have good Potential to date tricks and leech them, or use their looks in jobs. I can help her do something about her status ASAP, suggest career moves, social moves, or improving certain skills and in return, she'll be able to show her appreciation. This is what I call advising. In this case, I would be forfeiting some initial attributes and consider my time an investment. Free burgers in the meantime! I simply appreciate her doing what she can for me.

• Low/Medium Clout

The lowest qualifying category. They occupy very little of my time.

We are only able to do things that cost little, or nothing, to do. Low spending power means we can't go to the widest variety of venues, or go out so often. They will only meet me for the odd movie, regular meal, visit my home and bring small gifts like CD's, books, DVD's. The lower her Potential, the more sensible it is to meet at my home.

These hoes may also see me if I happen to pass through their place of work. I have one that works at a

DIY and furnishing superstore. I get twenty-five percent discount on everything. It's good to know people in strategic places. One at a car dealership could get me cheap servicing and discounted parts. Clothes shop, video hire, restaurant, salon, club, jewellers, the list goes on. That can add up to a lot of money staying in my pocket and effort saved. I've also been know to receive offers to help decorate, clean, garden for me and generally help out.

- **Medium Clout**

Next up it's employed hoes with reasonable salaries or status. They usually only call at my house to pick me up or drop me off. They can wine and dine me, take me for days out to amusement parks, activities, or places of interest. The odd weekend break and abroad in the long run. These are the type of expenses that are no problem. Reasonable presents would include basic clothing, mobile phones, and minor home furnishings. Also capable of contributing towards gym membership, movie subscriptions, insurance, jewellery, watches and home entertainment systems, items for the kitchen.

- **High Clout**

They do say the more money, the more naïve a person becomes. For someone wealthy, buying me something decent isn't going to be a big thing financially, but it could be emotionally. She will be able to take me for discerning weekends away and holidays abroad. They will be able to give premium gifts, such as couture clothing, gym membership, insurance, alloys, electrical goods, white goods, car sound system, home furnishings, porcelain veneers, and personalised number plates. The list is as endless as both of our imaginations.

Hoes holding an influential position within a company might offer me a good position and salary, not to mention the perks. But that's a minefield I shall expose in "Power Baiting" in due course. I avoid it.

Copping

Patience is a Fox's best friend.
Paradise

Ideally a hoe should, and will, always make the first move. She will Choose and Copp me. This I would classify as requesting my number and asking to see me socially. She may give all kinds of weird and wonderful excuses for obtaining it or seeing me, but nevertheless, she did so. Actions!

When they do this I am starting how I mean to go on. I'm being sought after. I have the Balance of Power and she is Choosing me strong. She knows she likes me more than I do her. I am immediately in the position to state and require my terms and conditions of engagement, my Contract. Whereas if I was not a Fox, I would be the one being made to conform to all kinds of terms and jumping through various hoops.

A hoe isn't going to do anything she can get me to do for her. I never initiate any form of contact. I'm more patient than women, and if the situation is that we are going to be in the same place repeatedly, there is no reason to go further than light Reciprocation. I watch her jock me on the quiet. She can stare or smile. She can say hi. She can chat to me briefly whenever she approaches me and initiates conversation. All I do is chill and Reciprocate until she can't tolerate it any longer and reaches out to me. This can range from minutes to months and months. It could even be a year or so. Believe me, if she has Waited all that time, she will be in appropriate condition for someone who has!

There are only three things within my control that I can do to bring fronting to a premature conclusion: improve my Front or Clout, go to the place she sees me less frequently, or for her to find out that I am going away for a long period of time. People front far less in a never-see-you-again situation. When I'm abroad most women don't even front, they come right at me, asking for some, like they're supposed to. It's like I'm the Pied

Piper. Conversely, if she sees me daily, the hoe will bide her time.

When they make their move, I chat a little as shown in stage two, below, then supply my digits as in stage three.

My mouth is like a fire door - only to be used in emergencies. I have written preliminary stages because there is a scenario in which I would make advances towards a woman. This is called "Taking Her to Court." It must be unlikely that we will meet again and she must have been allowed as much opportunity as possible to make a move first. This protocol also presumes that I am satisfied with what little circumstantial Evidence there is, that she is Choosing me. The amount of Evidence necessary for a trial is directly linked to the likely-hood of her bumping into me again. No chance = Minimal Evidence. Then I will Take Her to Court.

- **Taking Her to Court Part I**

At a Distance, Evidence Obtained, No Contact Made
& We Wouldn't Meet Again

I Wait until her eyes are locked on me, then look at her and beckon her over by silently motioning with my middle and index fingers. When she strolls over, I proceed to stages two and three.

If she does not go for it, it doesn't mean my Evidence was flawed. It tells me that they're going to be harder to break. They're used to tricks jumping through hoops and spoiling them. She's just a decent hoe. If she has good Potential, after she looks a good few more times I will repeat the motion.

Should she still not put one foot in front of the other, it will be the unluckiest day of her life. She will front less next time!

- **Taking Her To Court Part II**
- **She Initiates Contact Part I**

Close Range, Some or No Contact Made
& We Wouldn't Meet Again

When a woman strolls up to me and speaks first, it makes it all that easier to break into conversation. She gets full marks. But if I'm Taking Her to Court and have beckoned her over, or wish to Take Her to Court at close range - because she's stood close to me and she's silent - I would Wait for eye contact and smile lightly at her. I might say, "Are you not going to introduce yourself? Or, "Do you just like to look?" Or, "Don't you know it's rude to stare at strangers?" "So you saw me looking at you looking at me!" "How are you doing?" Or if she's sitting at the checkout, something like "It's nice and quiet today for you." Or "You look tired." Or comment on an item I am buying or something occurring like the till roll running out. Not even a question, and she'll start chattering like she's been marooned on a desert island for the last year if she's Choosing. Or, in a club, "Listen, if you think I'm going to try to pull you like all these shallow guys who aren't thinking with their brains, you're mistaken." Then go straight into something along the lines explained in the next section. What I say depends greatly on the hoe and the situation. Chat up lines: "How much does a polar bear weigh? Neither do I know, but it's enough to break the ice." are for tricks. I just talk straight up and sincerely to a hoe. Let her know what I'm about.

"You look as if you have something to say..."
The Kidd

Planning is fundamental to success. Lack of strategy is universally synonymous with failure. During uneventful times it is wise to prepare for eventful times. My mind is occupied thinking through "what if" scenarios wherever I am and analysing previous situations. Toying with approaches, responses and how to Fire-blast fronting.

Here's an example of what I do in cases where the woman initiates contact. A woman starts chatting to me in the supermarket, I watch for body language whilst analysing what she is saying. There is no other Evidence, except that she has invaded my personal space. She comments that the item I that have picked off the shelf is tasty. As we talk I Wait to see if she makes any conversation on a less formal level as I Reciprocate, to strengthen my Evidence. She doesn't, so to initiate the trial, I gently steer us off the dessert in my hand. "I never compromise on anything. I always get what makes me happy. What's life without the things we like?" A smile, followed by personal chat. By her reaction to a slightly more personal subject, I could review my Evidence. It also gave her more opportunity to make a move or submit stronger Evidence by expanding on our conversation. She still didn't, yet she responded well, so I commenced Court proceedings, as in section three.

This smooth transition from a formal to informal, informal to personal conversation is the key principle in these situations where I'm caught by surprise and need to Take Her to Court. This provides her with maximum opportunity to make a move on me, gives her some brain bait, and allows me to gauge any forthcoming Evidence as she reacts. I really test them out to the end of the conversation before I start talking phone numbers. Anything that could be construed as seeking her plants the seeds of trouble in her mind.

- **Taking Her To Court Part III**
- **She Initiates Contact Part II**

Closure When a She Expresses Desire for Further Contact, or When She is Fronting

In any case, wherever we are, I chat briefly, but unhurriedly. I lay down my Contract, time permitting. We have fun and get an impression of each other. I don't mention going out or her Clout, her appearance or any Front, except Emotional - her personality, if at all. A few minutes is ample. The shorter, the sweeter. What do most tricks do? Try and get as far as possible in no time.

She'll be intrigued; she'll have lots of unanswered questions, things to think about. Why don't I flirt, try to pull, try to impress her, act desperate, and look like everyone else? Mystery in itself is a motivation, it's exciting. As soon as she solves a man, a hoe will loose interest and seek a new challenge. I'm not Connect Four. I'm like a Rubik Cube that has had its stickers switched.

Meanwhile, I'm waiting to see if she asks me for further contact. I like to give her opportunities to do this, to see if she's buying, or not. A good way to create an opportunity is to respond at some juncture along the lines of, "Gosh, it would take me a long time to explain that to you." Or, "Well thank you, but you hardly know me yet." Or, "I could spend ages telling you about that."

After as little time as possible I make it apparent that I must leave and am bringing our encounter to a conclusion. If she's at her place of work, I let her know that I'm aware she has her job to do. In a club, that I know that we're both out with our friends. If in a shop, that I don't have much time. I focus on me having things to do, as well as her. I emphasise the value of my time. It's a nice way to prompt her to let me know she wants to be in contact in future. I may abruptly cut the chat off in mid-flow if she's getting into personal conversation. Tell her "Look, it's nothing you've said, I'm comfortable talking to you actually, but I really need to be somewhere." Or "I'm enjoying talking to you, but I just realised I'm going to be late. I wish I didn't have to go because..." It's easy to write down phrases, but I can't stress highly enough that my whole vibe, body language, tone, eyes, are much more important than words alone.

If she doesn't do the sensible thing, I continue to bring the chat to an end. Before I say goodbye, I ask her name, or ask her it again if she has already told me. It's a nice way of letting her know she has a chance with me. This is her final opportunity to make a move. I say bye, maybe that it was nice chatting, and move.

If the hoe is Choosing, but still backwards in coming forwards, I turn back towards her and push the issue. I state that we obviously don't really know each other, can't get to know each other here and now, and tell her (not ask) to write down, or take my number. "Put my number in your mobile and then we can continue, with a proper, unhurried conversation sometime. See if we hate each other or not." "I want to know more about those cakes you told me about, they sound delicious. So how are you going to tell me about them?" "Why don't you call me so you can give me more advice on…" "Listen, I need to go, but I don't see why we shouldn't continue our conversation another time." "Aren't you going to ask me for my number?" Or, "Let's stay in touch." I bless her with my digits, allow her to find a pen, or key them into her cell. Her writing as I dictate. I deflect any attempt by her to give me her number. "I'd rather we spoke when you wanted to." "No. I'd rather you contact me in your own time, when you have time to speak." "No, I never done that." I don't pause for a comeback - did you see a question mark back there? I immediately instruct her to call me for a chat, to get to know each other a bit more. See if my first impression of her is right or not. Then I'm gone like a twocked Supra.

There's an Engineering approach that I frequently use, where instead of telling a hoe to take my number down, I behave as if she already has it. This helps prevent her from trying to lay her digits on me. As I'm about to walk away, I'll advise her to give me a call. If she's Choosing, she'll then frown, "OK, but wait, I don't have your number do I, how am I supposed to do that?" So now she's asking me for my number. Just how it should be. Awww, how romantic!

At Mickey D's I had a cashier holla to a co-worker in the back. She looked at me and said excuse me. I said, tongue in cheek, "its not polite to yell in the customer's ear." She blushed and apologised again. I told her that wouldn't do, I needed her supervisor. She pleaded, ahh come on - I said I was sorry! I told her don't be sorry, make it up to me. She replied what could she do? Because she was Choosing me like crazy, I said take me for dinner. She said bet. I gave her my number and got the call.
Topchoice

Girl with her friend [Yelling from the kerb, half-joking. This being facilitated by Paradise's windows being down]: Give us a ride.

Paradise [pulling over to his side of the road]: I never ride in a car with a stranger. But it's up to you if you want to change that.

Girl [crossing the road with her friend]: How do you mean?

I mean I'm choosy about my friends. Listen, I have to be somewhere, but give me a call so I can get to know you a little and then we can see.

How can I do that? [Takes business card.]

Internet Copping

The internet is a useful, time-effective way to Copp. It's a unique, excellent way of getting to know a whole range of people who I would otherwise never bump into. I mean you are basically in someone's house with them. The same Copping principles apply wherever I am. The most important thing to me is minimising my time wasted, because it's so easy to on the net. Here are my SOPs.

Environment. If in chat rooms or forums, the first tactic is to be in a good Environment. I select a places with a good attendance and demographics. Sites that allow users to enter several rooms simultaneously are useful. In these I can also see the ratio of males and females in each room at a glance, allowing me to rule some places out of the equation. Incidentally, I have found the coolest time to connect is when there's a big football match on. Most males will be busy watching the match, and the ones on line are usually chatting about football.

I click to enter several rooms. Now I type something that will allow girls to decide to Choose me, or steer clear. I could type a very short note which discusses points like these... "Is there a caring, fun, deep, girl here?" "Who puts friendship first?" "Is there a down to earth girl with initiative, intelligence and emotional intelligence here?" At the end of each message I always type a call to action, "Whisper me/Private message me. No cyber pleaseeee!" Of course, like anything is this book, everyone's own persona and objectives would reflect in what they say. If in chat I can highlight the text and use the copy function. I can then paste and send it in each room consecutively with little effort.

This way women are coming to me, like they should be. I know that they are at least mildly interested, and have a degree of initiative, if they message me. They know I'm not trying to have any dirty cyber sex with them, so we can get chatting as in "Incoming Calls." As with face-to-face contact, I decide as early as possible who I'm going to put on "ignore" by assessing how hard they are Choosing me by going a little picky and playful on them for any reason that they provide, and seeing how keenly they comply. I then bring proceedings to a conclusion in mid-conversation in the same manner as "Taking to Court."

Requests for my mobile number are responded to by saying I need to get to know them a little more first or some sort of fun challenge. When hoes say that they will chat to me again sometime or they will keep a look out for me, I type, "I don't come on here regularly." I want a specific Invite, date and time. Only when I've said goodnight and they still don't ask for my email do I use my "Jedi mind-trick." I'll talk as if she already has my email address or number.

A small proportion of the hoes that take my email address will develop into long-term correspondences and Copps. It's therefore practical to maintain a brief profile on whom I've been chatting to. Its main function is to jog my memory and allow us to strike up immediate rapport without repeating ourselves. Perhaps some questions I would like to ask next time she contacts me. Ideas on how to proceed.

The following example is cut from a chat. In this short excerpt there's lots going on. The hoe's testing me on several levels, I'm checking her, killing flirting, defining myself different from tricks, I'm using repression to make her fold under the pressure of the conversation finishing, and there's a hint of Firing.

Paradise: It's late, I need to be up early.
Sue: Night hun.
Please.... [call me by my name], not hun. OK take care and have a nice weekend.
What you mean take care?
What you mean what you mean take care?
You're going just like that no email nothing all this chat well I never.
Oh.
Oh hahah.
????
Do you want to keep in touch or not that's all

Mail me
What ya mean mail me you are the man, mail me!
*****@******.com I shall reply to you.
*****@******.com. I shall reply to you lol
Forget it, how sexist are youuu? Look if you really genuinely want to be my friend don't treat me as some "guy."
You're taking it the wrong way silly you're not just some guy I'm trying to play hard to get lol
Take care. I know if you're bothered you'll write, if not you're not the nice person I think you are. Bye Sue [I log off immediately]

Another online resource is dating sites. The only legitimate ones are those advertised repeatedly in the mainstream media. Not those found in men's media.

I look at how I appear in the search results. The objective is to stand out... in a good way! As with chat-up lines, the secret is astoundingly simple: do not start acting in special, strange or gimmicky ways because of your insecurities. Just be yourself, be straight forward and present yourself in the best way. Someone will appreciate you. Here are some guidelines I use.

- Select three of the best from the biggest quantity of photos possible: pick them from the last three years, not the last few months. Consider if your friends and family have any more photos of you.

- Best photos show your face, especially eyes, with no shadow, in crisp focus, and are of medium or high resolution.

- Best photos are in warm daylight.

- Best photos are outdoor photos with only natural backgrounds. No distractions or negative information. Sky, greenery, sea, flowers, lake. Most of the background is to be cropped out of the photo, so you are the focus, and so that you can be seen in detail on a small computer screen. But the small piece of unfocused background around you is also important.

- Best photos will probably not be of you staring straight at the camera like you are standing in a police line-up.

- If you are taking photos, always take lots, so you can delete the milk and keep the cream. The more milk you make the more cream at the top. Read about portrait photo taking tips online.

Some websites display search results, or suggestions, in order of those who were last active, so by taking a few seconds several times a day to log in and out I am able to increase my visibility.

Writing a profile is very personal: as with chat-up lines, if you try to appeal to everyone, you appeal less, and you are not being a Real Man. A profile has to be real, down to earth, fun, and neither too heavy or too light: I put in it a friendly salutation, facts about my outlook in life, some personal values, and things I enjoy doing, especially things that can be done as a couple. I also mention things that I'm curious about. I mention things I've not done that I would like to. I write no more than two or three short paragraphs.

My writing concludes with a call to action. An invitation or provocation to initiate contact. Perhaps a fun or interesting question I'd like an answer to, or an opinion on. Or I ask a question about the reader. Or I claim that I know a fair bit about a serious or fun subject and say that I will answer any questions on it. I want to make the reader smile, feel welcome, and make it as easy and comfortable as possible for someone to message me.

Incoming Calls

You can influence someone as much as you know them.
I know hoes better than they know themselves.
I'm an enigma to them. A fixed Rubik cube.
Paradise

The phone rings. By calling me up, or initiating further contact with me, the hoe is accepting my Contract. I consider I have Copped as soon as she asks me out. She may already have amending or replacing my Contract on her agenda, but she has agreed to it for now. She has Chosen me.

Our initial phone conversation will be our first long conversation. We're friends. We have fun and a cool chat. I leave alone the subjects of feelings and Emotions between us, sex in general and meeting each other. She'll bring them up when she wants to badly enough. Throughout the book you will notice that I allow repression to mushroom desire, which will help hoes to cease fronting, and maintains the Balance of Power.

As Sweet runs down in Iceberg's autobiography, I want to know her full history. Everything that happened since she popped out of her mother, if she can remember that far back. It's quite natural for me to really get to know people deep. Superficial, mundane conversation is necessary from which to link and progress onto deeper subjects, but it's secondary. We don't linger on it. People can talk about the weather, what they ate for dinner and sport to anyone. I'm on that "Other Level." I try to enable her to establish an emotional connection with me as soon as possible. I'm exploring and connecting on a deeper level, an Emotional and Clout level. I'm interested in how she feels. What she wants in life. How she felt when this and that happened. What she took from it. What has really affected her. Reflections on her life. Her relationship with her parents. What the last thing she cried about was. How her relationships have started, progressed and ended, especially to ascertain why she Chose her

81

boyfriend and what caused her to top Choosing him. What she likes and dislikes about her current situation. We chat freely. How she arrived at certain decisions, expressing her opinions on any subject. Aspirations, fantasies, dreams. What she would like to experience that she has never done before. Where does she want to be in five years? Where she would like to travel. What her perfect holiday, weekend, or home would consist of. What book, song, or movie scene is her favourite and why. I move in any direction she wishes. I don't try to be what a she wants, but she may go for some of my virtues more than others. It's like a car in a showroom. Some clients might look at its engine, interested in its acceleration, others will be concerned about its safety features and warranty. Yet others will find the leather and veneer interior appealing. But the car remains the same.

Besides building good rapport, allowing us to genuinely get to know each other and promoting an Emotional link between us, this information will tell me a great deal about how she ticks. You can only influence someone as much as you know them. It tells me how to deal with her. About her character. It's invaluable. I begin to assess her motivations, her desires, although I don't do so directly. A hoe won't always consciously tell me what she really wants deep down. A Fox will know what she wants even when she doesn't!

If her ex treated her like rubbish, but she still loved him, or sounds still a bit lovey-dovey about him, or she tried to cling on at the end of her previous relationship, I know I can put my foot down more with her. If she's had only short term, casual sex relationships recently, and gets bored with people quick, I would ensure that it takes her longer to get to know me, to get Intimate with me. The shit reads like a Ladybird book.

I assess a hoe's Potential as accurately as possible. Now many will downplay their financial situation. Others may also complain about being in debt, or care less about debt, but one has to bear in mind that they are in debt because they don't have a problem with spending money when they want to, not because their ethos is to spend responsibly. They would rather shop than pay off their accounts. This is their own business at first, although I would never allow someone to put herself into financial difficulty and I actively encourage my women to be solvent and debt free. Why give away money to a bank? Lastly, I like to let her chat a while in order for us to get to know each other, but it's good form to be the one who brings the conversation to a conclusion. I restrict the first, and any future scheduled calls, to between ten minutes and an hour in duration. Always shorter than she wants them to be.

Once she starts taking me out, the bulk of conversation is transferred to date situations: phone calls are less frequent. This adds incentive to take me out to receive more of my attention. When our time expires, I round off the call by telling her it was nice getting to know her some more, I have to go do something and to let me know, give me a quick buzz, or arrange by text to chat again. She's already aware that I won't be available at her leisure.

I allow her to continue calling me or bumping into me until she's racking her brains about going out with me. Patience is a Fox's best friend. Her only possible course of action, besides trying to manipulate me into asking her, which she'll fail to do, will be for her to make a move. She doesn't ask, she doesn't get. Every day that passes until then is a top-up on my Balance of Power. Last week a hoe that's been dialling my number, when scheduled, for over four months asked to meet me. She's plotted me a generous sized estate in her mind for a long, long time to come.

The Other Level

You can be as romantic as you please about love;
but you mustn't be romantic about money.
George Shaw

In "Front" I described the necessity for an Emotional affinity between a hoe and I. Sex is an abundant commodity, therefore to really tighten a relationship we must take it to the "Other Level." There should always be more than twice as much Emotional Intimacy as any Sexual Intimacy. I tunnel deep into a hoe's mind, like "Mr Driller." I stimulate her brain more than her body. I keep the kingsiza out of her, and on her mind. Being a Fox is not a sex contest.

My superiority, balance, trustworthiness, mature composure, conversational ability, enthusiasm to understand others and deep nature encourage a hoe to open up to me, expose her private persona and form some Emotional link to me. This intangible connection is not necessarily equal on both sides. I'm not going to trip in an unrealistic way over a hoe, or reveal the intricacies of my Emotional history, but I speak freely on Emotional subjects.

It is important not to pollute our world by bringing into it everyday stress and concerns too frequently, or for prolonged periods. Wouldn't it be would be a mood-killer if a lover asked if your ill pet was recovering, or if you had a good day at work, during foreplay? Likewise, one must be sensitive to preserving a predominantly pleasurable and dreamy everyday atmosphere and not breaking the spell.

I allow the hoe to go as deep as she wants, but I never try to coax information out of her. Hoes often remark, "Oh I can't tell you what I was thinking the other night." Or, "There's something I want to say, but I'm not sure if I should. Maybe not." I don't fall into their stone-age trick-trap. Like Too $hort raps, "She wanted to play games, so I taught her mine." I say "Sure, no problem. I

85

understand." I let them bottle it up inside until, eventually, out it comes naturally.

A hoe may talk to me about poignant events in her life. Discuss inner issues, things relating to them, normally private thoughts. Whereas fine details of my personal history are mostly private. I talk in general about Emotions, life, and about the deeper things I love in our world. In particular, I have a fascination of storms and the ocean. To me they represent the raw, uncontrollable, wild, powerful unfathomable beauty and magic of the forces of nature. We might discuss loneliness, and how one can feel happy and be smiling in a crowded room, yet in their heart they can feel unfulfilled. How staring at the night sky provokes thoughts. We talk as I described in "Incoming Calls." She may like to watch the sea, love the wind, or be afraid of the dark. We'll talk about how things make her feel and what memories or thoughts they evoke. The past and the future. I enjoy deep conversation.

I would describe the Other Level in several ways. All five senses become Emotionally receptive in another dimension. Things become Emotionally charged. A hoe might get stomach-ache when I'm gone. When she's with me, she's buzzing off chemicals her body is releasing into her system. Touch is not simply perceived as touch; the warmth of my body may feel like Emotions transferring into her. My voice has an effect on her. She catches a whiff of the scent I wear in a store and gets and get heart palpitations. This is where we have something between us. A vibe that puts us on an Other Level from everybody else.

Signs of a deep Emotional connection usually come in the form her explaining that she thinks of me when she listens to a particular song. She smelt my aftershave in a shop, or on somebody and thought of me. She says that she believes fate brought us together and tries to connect things. They talk about the compatibility of our star signs or focus a lot on similarities. They try to get me to leave any kind of little object behind when I split. They have printed every email I've sent them, don't erase my text messages, or they have a connection to me through gazing at the night sky or the ocean. I can also tell by their breathing if I move in close range to them, or by the voltage in their eyes.

Now it's time to discuss the four-letter word. I may agree that there's a vibe between us, that we connect on some levels. There's something good between us. That she made my heart beat faster when she gave me the golf clubs or was extremely kind. That I like how we're open with one another. I'm not talking about being or saying I'm "in luuuurrrvel" I'm not. She can say it more often than a Wimbledon umpire, if she likes. I could never fall in "love" with a hoe, by definition. I might love her in a different way because how she is and what she does for me. This doesn't change the fact that hoes are dispensable and fundamentally unethical people who only behave when there is the necessity to. I'm not talking about getting Emotionally dependent on a hoe. She very well may do with me though. What I want is for her to feel she needs me. She probably wants to feel that too. Near unconditional Emotional dependency. Her mind will be totally gone! She'll be mine.

Saying the word "love" (apart from being dishonest because she's bound to misinterpret a Fox's meaning) would mean, "Here's the Balance of Power." It'd be like Christmas for her. She would think she had something of worth to me to be able to utilise, threaten or withdraw in order to exploit me.

I mentioned Emotional dependency above. Here's what I mean by the term. If an individual is balanced, mature, has come to terms with themselves and put their life in perspective, emotional dependency can be near impossible. This often comes from a solid family background, or from being single and independent for a length of time, especially following a relationship. They will be reasonably content as a person, not excessively needy of affection from someone else for their happiness. Therefore they will assess a person and a relationship more rationally. They will not disregard Behaviour or compromise their own standards to the same extent.

Someone who is less balanced has a high likelihood of becoming Emotionally dependent on someone. They may have been in an abusive, sexless or hurtful relationship, they may have unresolved issues from their childhood. Low self-image, insecurity, loneliness and ego seem to be the most common characteristics that these people want to use someone to shield themselves from. This type will always cry if they talk deep enough about their particular issues and can bring some baggage with them, maybe bad behavioural habits they need to stop. When I see irrational behaviour, or I am told about some irrational behaviour she did, I am patient and take the time to explore and understand the reasons why. This does not mean I will sympathise with someone acting in a bad way in my presence. There's no excuse to act up with me. But I can empathise and get to the issue with them, get them to recognise what is happening and work to resolve it with them if they will make the effort.

Email: I think you're right. I'm moving too fast and I shouldn't. This is cool just as we are, so even though I have a really warm feeling inside me it's probably best if we just keep it at this level. I know me and I imagine I'd be craving for more. I must learn to control myself more but my imagination always just gets carried away. My mind has labelled you as some kind of manly, sensual, powerful, sensitive, warm person and naturally I am drawn to you as if there's something bigger there. When really it's my mind working overtime. It's because I want to find someone who absolutely blows my mind and I just can't think straight because of them. I have been remembering what you said yesterday about touching someone's hand and feeling more than just the actual touch. That just sums it up to me, there has to be an extra something. I have been in search of that extra thing for so long. I have never really ever had that to the depth that I want it.

Firing

*Whatever makes a person feel happy possesses an
equal Power over them to render them unhappy.
Between these extremities lies my Power.*
Paradise

I don't initiate conflict. I conclude it. I don't compete for
the Balance of Power. I permanently possess it.
Certainty or doubt of one's own Power is not only a red
or green light to being tested, it predetermines if a
confrontation will result in success or failure. The term
"Firing" refers to the procedure of abruptly confronting a
hoe with the fact that she isn't mine until she acts right,
or unless she acts right. Leaving her with a clear
ultimatum of Bolting or Behaving, if she tests that far.
    Permanently leaving hoes with Potential is like burning
money. I don't Package to hoes "Never call me again." I
convey, "Don't call me again unless you..." Firing simply
weeds out the Performers from the lames. If a hoe isn't
respecting me, I either want her to act right or to stop
wasting my time. Both are good results, but of course
the result with the most benefits optimal. I always want
a hoe if she's sweet, but I never need a hoe who isn't.
Firing conclusively answers the most important question
in a hoe's head. All the information she has absorbed
until that point tells her that I don't need her. Hoes
create a cold war for the Balance of Power. I'm a nuclear
threat looming over her world night and day. It deters
conflict in the first place. She, rightly, may seek proof of
my capability. And will do again any time she hopes that
the Balance of Power has swung. So this is the real
unsaid issue her and I are dealing with whenever she
confronts or tests me.
    Similar to a real life nuclear holocaust scenario, as
soon as I embark into "launch" mode (relationship
terminated mode) the hoe will want to come back to the
table and re-negotiate. Except because I'm indifferent to
pressing the button, there is no negotiation. Ever been in
a relationship and suddenly one of you is deciding

whether to break up, and the other is Choosing strong, especially Emotionally Dependent? What does the other person do? They flip into a warp, a mind state where they compromise; they'd do anything to keep the other. But should the red-alert signals be insufficient, if she calls my bluff, I have the ultimate weapon. And I'm immune to it, remember!

Firing hoes is one of the best things I can do. It's SOP. Every hoe needs to be Fired. I Fire some hoes several times before they Copp me! Now that's a strong Copp. I wait for any opportunity to terminate a hoe's Contract from the first time we meet. A situation will unfold where she will not acknowledge the Balance of Power. It doesn't matter how trivial. I have my principles. What may appear to the layman as perhaps a silly, unimportant, isolated incident lets a hoe know a whole lot about my standards and either increases or diminishes her respect. Tests that crop up include petty situations where a hoe pesters me non-stop to do something such as show them something or do a task she can do herself. She may remark "Whatevver!" disrespectfully, like she's on Jerry Springer, when we chat. She may ask to try my watch on, for me not to stand near a balcony edge, for me to call her at a certain time, to be tactile, flirt, and want to do undesirable things to me - even test some nail polish on me for fun.

Once I have said no, I treat her like a Gremlin after midnight. Finally, she may add some flirting or try a bullshit threat as a last attempt. If I cave in once, she'll turn nasty and do it again and again. No means no – and don't test me. She should never be rewarded for questioning my resolve. I never concede a point, unless I add it to her "Wish List" and eventually use it to Reward Behaviour. It would have to be seen as given on my terms. I always stand by what I say. The message gets through.

Silence is the most perfect expression of scorn.
George Shaw

The harder I am being Chosen, the easier I'm provoked to Fire. If we're not too tight, or if I think that it's sufficient, she will receive more preliminary visual or verbal warnings that she's turning me off her. That we're appearing incompatible, and will withdraw my Intimacy first.

My blood turns into liquid nitrogen as I instantly recoil like she's got cholera, telling her sometimes verbally, and always via my actions, that she can't possibly aspire to be my friend if she doesn't act like one. I could state "I'm not comfortable with doing that." "I don't want to be told you'll call me presuming this and that. Just wait 'till you decide you are definitely going to and let me know a few days in advance." Often, "launch mode" can be mimed. Placing immediate physical distance between her and I, withdrawing the long-term level of Intimacy. My frostbitten face, me simply leaving or cutting her off the phone calmly without warning, my silence or economical use of words can be an adequate deterrence, and she'll acknowledge Power. When I cut off my mobile they call back my voicemail distraught, unsure whether the reception was lost, but their Balance of Power gauge is on red so they handle me like Ming porcelain. If they ask me if my network cut me off, I ignore their Trojan Horse question. I continue talking and ask them what they want, putting them on the defence.

Which is stronger and more powerful: your determination to end the conflict, or your fear of loosing the relationship? In order to triumph over conflict, you must understand thoroughly your motivations, for they describe your destiny.
Sun Tzu

Hoes can flip my thermostat like Dr Jekell and Mr Hyde. Just as I allow hoes to get closer to me if they are sweet, if they go sour I get icy. By icy I mean composed, logical, emotionless, intolerant and uncompromising. I will talk firmly and briefly. I'm always in control. I'm never reactive.

I will not be provoked into any problematic or compromising position. Even if a woman did something malicious to my property or me, all she would get from me is the bare minimum of self-defence as I quickly get away from the place. From that moment she would never be able to see or contact me again. But she will receive a visit from the police.

Hoes have no Power to raise my temperature and bring out childish, illogical, insecure, destructive, uncontrolled Emotion in me. Just as tempestuous weather is incapable of exposing the sensitive inner of flora, naturally protected within its calyx.

There is no avoiding conflict. It can only be
postponed to the advantage of others.
Niccolo Machiavelli

I only check a hoe on one issue at a time. This is so because I always check her instantly whenever she tests, so there can never be more than one issue that needs checking at any moment in time. This is advantageous because I am always checking her from a position of strength. I am not asking her to change Behaviour that I have previously accepted. This would display fear, an absence of Power, and undermine its importance. She also has to weigh loosing me against correcting a single issue. The three essentials when Firing and checking a hoe are:

- **The Return Contract Clause**

I emphasise the one issue that will make her eligible to be mine. I question her capacity to meet my standards because of this issue. I make it crystal that it is the difference between having me and not having me.

I Package to her that we are together because I thought she might have been able to be a close friend. Maybe I saw something in her, she seemed sweet in certain instances, but I'm disappointed, offended or hurt that she's not acting like one right now. If she says that she opposes my Contract, I may say, "That's the biggest turnoff to me. If you aren't X, I can't be friends with you." Or "If you can't be bothered, neither can I." By doing this, I'm really telling her how to act when she returns. I'm setting out a "Return Contract Clause."

• The Stable Door Is Always Open.

I Package to her that she does have the Potential to be with me, but only if she wants to act right. My stable door is always open to Top Performers, always closed to someone who brings problems with them. She can return, conditionally. It's Choose or loose!

I might leave her with words ringing in her ears like, "Don't call me unless you plan on being nice to me." "I want you if you are that woman you said you were, the friend that you seemed to be, but if you aren't, then I'm obviously not your type." "I know that if I'm wrong about you, you'll call me. If not then we'll know that the things you have said to me aren't true and we needn't talk." Works like a Swiss watch. "Look, you either act like a mature, caring friend or you stop wasting my time. Now what's it to be?" Or, "I have people who I don't consider friends who behave nicer to me than you are doing." Paradise has now left the building! "Look, I can't possibly speak to you properly until you show me you're sorry." Then, "Telling me you're sorry is one thing. Do you intend show me that you really mean you're sorry? You don't know? In that case we have nothing to speak about until you do." A classic response to "First Contact."

• Conciseness

Not turning my statement into a debate or prolonged dialogue. I'm not asking, I'm telling. Time is of the essence: Firing is done as swiftly as possible, part of its strength is its lightening speed.

Conversing with a hoe about something to which there can be no response other than yes or no is like telling her there is the option to negotiate. Before I reach the

Firing stage, I may respond to a calm remark, but only by swiftly emphasising my other two points. But when Firing I ignore any attempt to draw me into a discussion or distract us from the issue. She will take any willingness to discuss things as a sign of weakness. It's counter productive. I maintain focus on the urgency and importance of the only issue we have left to talk about!

My reader, I can't find words to really describe to you how well a hoe Behaves after she's been Fired. Nuclear fallout has devastating effects. The radiation doesn't dissipate easily. If I hadn't already reversed her, a "Rules," "wine-and-dine-me," type manipulator will become a Top Performer overnight. Hoes have even sent me cash and cards in the post after I've excommunicated them. They think of doing things for me that *I* haven't even thought of!

Let's cut to some real life examples of me in action. There are more in the Rendezvous chapter.

Emma: Can you meet me outside my work?
Paradise: [in a calm but firm voice throughout] I don't understand why you're asking me that.
I'll meet you there. It would be nice to meet you there. It's easier.
You can't get to the Westfield Mall? You invited me there.
I said down town, you said you preferred Westfield, so I'm fine to go there. I know where it is, yes. I can follow the signs, but I've never been from work before.
I've never been there from your work before. Emma, you said that you are able to find your way, yet you are still asking me?
Yes.

Click! Deadline! Five minutes later comes the second call. After it rings for a long minute...

Emma: Have we just had our first argument?
No, I never waste my time arguing. Look, I'm driving. You can call me quickly in half an hour if you need to talk.

Thirty minutes later...

Emma: Hello. I'm so upset, [Paradise] I'm crying here,
can we be friends again?

Only you know how you are going to be with me. I
accept people how they are. If people act like good
friends, then I have time for them. If not, I use my
time wisely.

I'm sorry, I was only joking with you, you know. I wasn't
serious. I don't know how you could think that.

I asked you in no uncertain way and you said yes. I
only have time in my life for the best people I can
surround myself with. If people turn out not to be,
I try not to be disappointed at my misjudgement.
I'm very sensitive to how people are with me. It
means I appreciate good friends and am also
quickly hurt when I notice someone isn't one.

I'm sorry, we've got our wires crossed, I was only
kidding. I'd never do anything to hurt you. If you still
want to go, I'll see you there on Wednesday.

Invites

I always allow three options. My way, time stands still until its my way, or the highway.
Paradise

I honestly can't remember the last time I asked a woman out. Maybe I was sixteen. Once she has taken me out a few times and a hoe knows what to do if she requires my company, things tend to run like an S Class. New Copps can be quite sexist or set in their ways to begin with. They're still catching their bearings with me. A hoe may kick some blatant hoe-to-trick shit to provoke me to trick. Such as, "Well, you not going to take me out? It's your turn to ask me out. Would you take me for dinner? I like to be wined and dined." Or try to camouflage it a little. "Oh honey, when can we meet? Where do you think we should go?"

These statements signify that her desire is stronger than mine, and she knows it. She's brought up the subject. This is exactly what I want. However blunt or tactful a hoe is with me, I respond to her bearing in mind how strongly she is Choosing me. I'd retort briefly to manipulative comments by including something along the lines of what follows.

"First it's your turn."

"Actually I was thinking about you taking me for lunch at..."

"Don't you think you wouldn't be able to take me somewhere new or fun that I've not been? That would be really fun to do."

"Let's not do all that boring unoriginal stuff. I like surprises, surprise me! You said you are quite different/romantic/thoughtful person and I liked that."

"Why not show me that place you mentioned, it sounded like fun and it's something different."

"Let's not play games, if you want to go out, just prepare, plan and propose something, and something original too. I'm tired of the same places."

"Next time you go to X you must take me with you!"

"I like a person to get to know me at their own pace and ask me out only when they feel comfortable doing so. Of course you like to know too, so I'm telling you. Let me know if you would like me to come out with you and where to. I find that to be much more of a compliment than words ever could be. There's nothing worse than people who play games and aren't open with me, or being asked out, then asked where we should go."

"Well I don't take people out, I'm not looking for a date, but if you would like me to come out with you somewhere, sometime, plan something and let me know. I'm too busy to do so too. I prefer to be asked out, because then I know that the other person really wants to be in my company. I don't ask people out because I don't expect everybody in the world to like me, but I like it when people show me that they do. Friends don't wait for each other to ask them out. A mature adult doesn't play games. I'd never go out with someone who wasn't both those things."

"Listen, there are people who accept what happens and what's offered in their lives. But a real woman chooses what she wants, controls her life and shapes her own destiny. Fate will only lead a horse to water. I only have time for mature, thoughtful, independent people. I like people with intelligence and initiative around me. It makes so much difference to me if someone shows me, proves to me what they say and how they feel. Let me know what you have in mind and we can see."

A hoe can point out that I seem to want her to play a "male" role by taking me out. "You're coming across quite naive. The world doesn't break down into men and women. It brakes down into two kinds of individuals. Coulda-shoulda-wouldas, and those who make things happen in their lives. Take a look around and you will see only one type is synonymous with success. From Madonna, Margaret Thatcher and Lil' Kim to Lady Diana."

"I'm not stupid enough to stand here holding this phone to my ear whilst you talk to me like this. I'm not interested in dating. I'm not interested in treating women like an incapable subspecies. I am interested in having good friends. And if you have a problem with treating a male with respect then you don't sound my type. You either want to be friends or you don't. Now which is it to be?"

After checking the hoe casually in passing conversation or wording her icily if an extreme case, I don't pause for a comeback. I take for granted that my statement is accepted, perhaps ignore a feeble comeback, and proceed immediately onto a new topic, or bring our conversation to a normal, abrupt end to really sponge up that Power. Firing is not my only defence against hoeing. Repression is a beautiful thing. I will never ask a hoe out, so there is only one way for her to meet me. Being a Fox is about demand exceeding supply. I never expand on her booby-trapped remarks about going out. If she pushes the issue after my response and tries to make a conversation out of it, I'll immediately Fire her. I always allow my hoes options. My way, time stands still until it's my way, or the highway.

A hoe may kick some, "Where you going? Oh, can I come with you? Oh, I go there. I'm not far from there." nonsense. There is no way I would agree to meet a hoe under any other circumstance than her specifically wanting us to get together. If that wasn't the reason and focus of it, we're better off doing our own thing until she feels that way. I find it offensive and unflattering. I don't see people out of convenience, coincidence or on the off chance. I explain so and leave it in her hands if she wants to arrange something. It simply lets her know she's dealing with a Real Man. It really steals the wind from their sails when I inform them that I've recently visited their part of town, too.

Even if a hoe asks me out straight away on her first or second call, I like to get to know her a little more first. I tell her that, and to ask me again the next time we speak, as I will have got to know her more by then. Likewise, the first time that she suggests that we spend a weekend away together, I always advise her that it sounds nice, I like that idea, but we can discuss it next time we go out. This is called "Wait Training." It does wonders for her mind state. I'm not going to go out with her just because she's ready. She can Wait until I am. I don't wish to go out with a hoe when she desires me. I require her to be far beyond that!

If she states that she wants to front - sorry, I mean be strictly friends - great. That saves me lots of work. That's what I've been saying to her all along. One day she might remark, "I have an idea. You know I love spending time with you and you said that you like to be able to relax and get to know each other without distractions in comfy surroundings? And it seems like our time together is always too short. Well, I thought if I took us away for a weekend or a holiday together we'd have just that. But tell me if you think I'm being too forward or you think it's a bad plan. I don't want this to come across as if I'm trying to make a move on you. Everything will be above board. We will have separate rooms of course. Our friendship is more important than anything and I would do nothing to jeopardise it."

I don't get mislead about intentions being non-sexual, or provoked into pushing for sexual behaviour or sexual talk. I go along with it. It's really exactly the same as saying she will take me away for a weekend and we will be in the same bed, just that she is stressing she understands that we are both single. Words are just words, I always observe actions. When she starts giving me head whenever I allow her to, I will have a private smile about what she said. So regarding a claim of just being friends, she still has to take me out, do me favours, if she wants to be friends. Sex is invariably far lower on my Wish List than a hers. All I want is what's at the top of mine.

When she does get around to asking me out, I decide what I will accept. I start how I intend to go on. She's likely to propose a venue of the same calibre that I have mentioned other hoes take me to, or that she knows I prefer. If her Potential prevents her from doing so, she will attempt to come as close as she can. My preference is for a good Cordon Bleu, Haute Cuisine standard restaurant, or something fun and of worth. I ensure hoes know that I don't like pubs, fast food joints, and bars. I don't go out for drinks, I dine. I don't go to swimming pools, I go to water parks. I don't sleep at motels. I stay at four or five star hotels.

Only if I have absolute Power - if I'm being Chosen harder than quantum physics - will I command a hoe like a General. Otherwise I never ask a hoe to do anything for me. I never suggest a venue or activity unless asked for my preferences, or unless she has made a suggestion first. If I dislike what she proposes, I have no qualms about refusing, pointing her in the right direction and letting her know what would be nice. It's not as if she's going to change her mind. I tell her my preferences about the kind of place it should be, or name a cinema, activity, restaurant, musician who is touring, hotel, resort, country or city. Nothing more. I don't know details. It is for her to offer and plan. She must take the initiative and make telephone calls if necessary. Do research. Go and buy Condé Nast Traveller, The Lonley Planet books, The Good Food Guide. Get the Red Letter Days catalogue and The Leading Hotels Of The World book. Make the effort. Then she can offer again. I'm not going out to please her. Anyway, she'll be pleased that I have high standards. The ultimate man, the ultimate relationship, belongs hand in hand with the ultimate surroundings. You know, like how the Queen believes everything smells of fresh paint.

It is wise to allocate dates to weekday or Sunday evenings. Fridays and weekends are for myself, only infringed upon if decent overnight breaks or all-day activities are agreed. I always agree to "around" a time, I'll say "See you eight-ish." I never promise to arrive on the dot, I take life easy, it's not a military operation.

There may be several near misses during Incoming Calls concerning going out together. I patiently Wait for a specific suggestion that we go out, or for her ask me out correctly. Once on this topic of conversation, she may not clearly ask me to come out with her. It may be more vague than that. My Packaging of specific personal pronouns and verbs is important here, as in all situations. I always refer in conversation to me going out with her, her taking me somewhere, I'll come with her. I might say it was nice of her to ask, or that it was a nice suggestion and she has taste. I'll trust her judgement on the choice of venue. I'm reinforcing that it is her who made the move. She is requesting my company.

Should I receive a general, non-specific offer, "Will you come to see me? Would you come out for dinner? I bet you wouldn't come on holiday with me, would you?" I answer that it sounds nice but I don't know. I need to know more about where before I could say. I'll be able to answer her fully when I know the full details. This shows that I'm not going out merely for company or to get into her good books, I'm not desperate, I have standards, and that consideration must be given to my desires.

I'm not some trick. I'm extra ordinary; I don't fit into a hoe's day-to-day, mundane life situations. Seeing me must be special. She may have to go out of her way. She can't just mould me and slot me in nicely. I never accept Invitations to parties, places of work, group social occasions or any events that she would be attending, irrelevant of my company. I'm always the centre of her attention, it's always just the two of us. She may have to reorganise her schedule for me, to fit into my life. Things you have made an effort to obtain you appreciate more.

Hoe's homes are utterly OFF LIMITS. The closer her index finger comes to touching my front doorbell, the more of a Fox I am. I'll come out; she doesn't come inside on early dates. I'll explain visits in the "Top Performance" section. If she isn't picking me up from my doorstep, the pick up spot or venue should be as local to me as possible. An exception would be an attraction not to be found nearby, or something of high value to me. I'm busy *and* putting myself out, don't forget.

On future outings, I avoid repeating our Rendezvous location. Always seek new places and new experiences. I tire of repetitive dates. These qualities also provide benefits from a Power aspect. Being away from familiar Environments is a sound principle because she will anticipate, enjoy and remember her experiences as more special and with a higher degree of excitement. Her mind will be occupied. She will not be able to put Invites on auto-pilot and get bored and spend time on manipulative thoughts.

Rendezvous

"It's okay, I'll take care of this one."
"Do you see me reaching for my fucking wallet?"
Film: Payback

I never arrive early for a date. I try to materialise within fifteen minutes of the pre-arranged time. This broadcasts all the right messages and puts me deeper into her mind.

In the event of being very late for some unexpected reason, I don't break my neck, sit stressed, sweaty, in car jams or rush dangerously. My women know that if I'm not there on time that there must be a reason. I have said I'll be there so I shall be there. I never break my word. She can contact me on my mobile if she can be bothered to.

If tested on my punctuality, I don't apologise or justify being delayed. I state she should appreciate realistically that I'm a busy guy and we live in a world of infinite, unpredictable variables and not everything is in our control. What is important is how we are when we are together. If she's concerned for me, cool, if not I'll point her selfishness out real quick. Likewise, if my hoe was ever late - and this hasn't happened yet - I'd never let her roll up and spot me Waiting for her. I'd return in fifteen minutes. If I had no word by then, I would leave sharpish. Upon her subsequent arrival she will understand that I'm not to be toyed with and presumably call me up. If she let me know she was on her way, but late for a valid reason, fine. I know she's Choosing me and after a quick apology we need not waste time on it.

As a rule, hoes never see the interior of my car, unless they have earned the privilege to do so (see Rewarding Behaviour.) She's an able bodied adult: with or without her own vehicle, she should meet me where we're going. She comes to me. It's good form. If she doesn't feel like that, she needs some time to develop that feeling! If you see me in a car with a hoe, you can bet I'll be in the passenger seat of that car. When we meet then travel onwards elsewhere, my woman chauffeurs me. If she hasn't got wheels, it's usually a taxi or public transport. This becomes routine, but initially I divert her from my ride by honestly stating that I have had enough driving to the Rendezvous. I don't feel like driving, and that I simply like her to drive me. In an area she is familiar with, I also explain that I prefer us to concentrate on conversation rather than us both messing around navigating. If tested, I could retort "Are you going out with me or my car?" Or, "You should know how I am by now, I am laid back, I don't like having to drive." Or, "You know I don't like to drive, it's not something I enjoy and I don't do things I don't enjoy." Or, "I want you drive."

When I am in people's company, or busy, I like to have a certain degree of privacy and to enjoy whatever I'm doing without being disturbed. I switch off, or silence, my mobile, when we meet in order that I am not interrupted. Having an mobile means that I can be contacted when I want, not when others want. This has a double benefit because when I don't reply to texts, or hoes reach my voicemail, they presume that I am likely to be with somebody else, or very busy. When a woman is taking me out, she is treating me right, therefore she receives my full attention, as I do hers. It's the only time she will receive it. When she's with me, she's my woman.

I reinforce the Contract's points consistently, all the time. Whilst out with girls, I continue to really get to know them as in Incoming Calls. There's so much to know. I will probably check things with her to add weight to my theories. And, of course, I have a good time. She's taking me where I want to go. She's acting right, so we can be friends and have fun.

When on dates, I allow hoes to lead the way into restaurants, up to shop tills, arrivals desks, in cinema queues and to assume an active role. It's best for her to lead the way up to these buildings too. I'm not sexist either: they can hold doors open for me. If I am ever in front, I would briefly hold the door, but not stand there like a porter. She will have normally made a reservation.

104

She speaks to the maitre d'. If there is a choice of table, I tell her which one I would prefer. I would rather not speak to staff at all. I follow her to the table. I select anything that appeals to me from the menu. I eat à la carte if I wish. I tell her what I will eat so that she can order for us both, but if not I'm fine. I let her take care of me. She's empowered, I'm in control.

Similarly, in shops I tell her what I want and she endeavours to get it, or allow her to take what I have picked out to the cashier. At hotels, it is not me that checks us in at reception. I'm sure that's why they have smaller feet - so they can stand closer to desks. She calls for room service. I like a woman to be thoughtful and attentive. Run my bath. Have my favourite drink waiting for me. Have that item I mentioned the next time she sees me. One of my Top Performers always buys the movie tickets before I even arrive. I never went for these passive, docile, incapable, hoes that you see in movies. I always liked the bad bitches like Onatop and the Cigar Girl in the Bond movies, because they have initiative, drive and are sharp. These other disabled hoes only ever lift a finger, like hesitantly, nervously throwing a vase at some-one's head in a panic if their man is getting fucking *killed* in front of them!

Another thing that is disappointing are sexist waiters and waitresses sliding bills in front of me. Even though my woman has asked for the bill. Despite that I have hardly looked at or spoken to them all night. Despite the fact that I'm not looking at anything but my woman, chatting to her, and she's probably looking at the bill in their hand.

Now with a good companion, she would just ask me to pass it over or ask for it to be given to her by the waiter. But in less than perfect situations the sexism can be countered by being sat forward with my arms on the table, forcing the bill to be placed further from my territory. Though this is only practical at smaller tables where there is little room either side of me. In any event, I never look downwards. I continue to look at her whilst we talk, and never have a peep at the bill. If she enquires how much it is, I pass it to her.

Sometimes I will only discover at this point that my date believes I'm going to start picking up bills, or part of them. She is merely pinching herself to check if she really does need to prove she's worthy of having me or if she is going to be getting everything for free and dominate another trick. So I consider it natural for her to want to check because I seem too good to be true. Is this a Real Man who has a spine and has options when it comes to who and how he dates? Remember: it is she who asked me out. In my eyes, going Dutch on things with a hoe is OFF LIMITS. I'm feeling like I'm going to go dizzy here, at just the thought of it. If she's cracking any fifty-fifty shit, I check that Behaviour immediately. I Fire her. If the Balance of Power is not assumed from the beginning, it becomes immediately difficult, and soon impossible to recover.

The sort of thing I'd come at her with would be "You asked me to come out with you. You'd be looking at me crazy too if I asked you out, then asked you to pay."

"I'm sorry, but I've never been asked out, then asked to pay towards it."

"Respect is important to me. I don't accept anything less from anyone with whom I associate. If taken out by a friend, one's friend doesn't turn around and expect them to pay for them. I would never spend my time in the company of anyone who I wouldn't consider to be a friend."

"I feel offended and disgusted. If we have to actually arrange to go Dutch then we shouldn't really be going out. If the cost of the bill is worth more to you than my company then, in my eyes, you're saying I'm not worth taking out. It's only a bill. What you're saying is I'm not even worth a plate of food."

"If money is an issue then you don't really like me. We should be the issue."

"I'm insulted that you confuse me with those men who pay bills thinking that they're buying more than just a meal. I don't buy friendship. If you're going out on a date, and some guy's crazy for you, I can understand that. But we're going out as friends. My time is valuable and I only like to spend it with people who know what they want, who place importance on what company they are in, rather than on material issues."

I could round it off with something like maybe it's our age difference: I'm used to a certain level of etiquette, I know she's mature enough to understand how I'm so sensitive, or maybe it's that we just move in different [social] circles, as if we're doomed. It'll incite her to conform to my standards and prove her compatibility with me. She perceives me as on a level above her. It should appear petty, unrefined and questionable of her pedigree, depth, and state of affairs that she wants to split the bill. I mean, do friends hit on you for money when they ask if you'd like a drink from the bar?

It's evident I've got the funds for a royal banquet. Paying is not in my realm of possibilities. I often don't carry money. At the end of the day, I always have the ace up my sleeve. Firing. I can put my foot right down and straight out state I was beginning to like getting to know her but it has been overshadowed, as it's appearing that we're incompatible due to her Behaviour. Even walk out. Leave her to pay. The ball is then in her court! This works a treat. They become Top Performers overnight.

Years ago, a hoe was testing me real hard in a restaurant over £25. I wasn't in the mood. I drew out a £50 note, showed it her and casually tore it along the middle. I tossed half over to her as I pointed out to her that this was what she was arguing about. I stood up and strolled out, leaving her with the bill. This was a very visual way of communicating that I have money and I have principles.

She came looking for me later on. She brought me back the torn half note. My relationship with a hoe is conditional upon her conforming to my standards. A hoe is trying to get what she wants from me, so if I get what I want from her, she'll be allowed to get some of what she wants and we're both going to be really happy and get along. It's in my interest. It's in her interest. She wants me. She takes care of me. She gets to go out with me and be mine. If she doesn't think I'm worth it, then she wouldn't do it. Simple.

The first time a hoe whisks me away, we may be in the same, or in separate rooms. If separate, I never knock on her door, call her, let alone go to her room for any reason. It's like Area 51. She must Wait for me downstairs in the in the lobby, or come to my door.

107

When she tries to tempt me, I tell her I'm going to my suite, I have something to do (perhaps raid the mini bar). If she wants to chat for a while, to come to my room in five, ten minutes time.

When it gets late, if we've been intimate or not, I tell her to return to her room. Often if I say, "Do you feel tired?" She will say that she does. She's thinking that I'm inviting her to stay, that she's going to rape me all night. I might say, "I am too, I'm going to clean my teeth. Then I'm going to bed." When I re-enter the room, they are usually in desperado-mode, really trying it on, failing to entice me as I say goodnight with a smile. I dampen any advances as shown in the "Intimacy" chapter.

I dictate what time I get up. Always seems to be later than women want! I usually have her come and knock on the door to wake me up in the a.m. then call out that I'll meet her downstairs for breakfast, or she can come in and order it to my suite. When we're staying in the same room, we could be sleeping in the same, or separate beds in early days. Rooms with two doubles are quite common and are often no different in price. If I want to leave sleeping in the same bed on her Wish list, I say that I'm more comfortable sleeping alone in my bed once we are ready to actually sleep: I must have a good night's sleep without being knocked and I like lots of space. She doesn't decide which bed, or which side of my bed she's going to sleep on. In fact if she tells me, I have her sleep on the opposite side.

Just because we're in the same bed, or same room, it doesn't have to mean we get fully Intimate. I Reward Behaviour, not misbehaviour, or doing nothing in particular. I'll cover this situation more in due course.

If we're not that Intimate yet, she goes to the bathroom to change, whilst I change in the bedroom. My belongings get priority in the wardrobes, the cabinets. I decide when we go to sleep. She arranges the wake-up call. She turns the light off.

Like showbusiness, it is always best to leave an audience wanting more, rather than letting them eventually decide they have had enough. This applies to Intimacy, to time Rendezvous and also keeps conversation a bit intriguing.

I avoid flooding the conversation with excessive information, which is something under-confident people often do. Once we exit the restaurant, attraction, or cinema, I wrap up the evening. Once we have returned from the airport, we immediately go our separate ways. This principle applies universally.

If a hoe ever looks at her watch or mentions going soon, it means she's had too much of me, I split ASAP. First I indicate that I'm about to go. Any time with me from then onwards is like an encore. I would always rather spend two hours less with them than one too many. I keep most Rendezvous to about three, four hours in duration. The only way she can get me for longer is by doing more. Whisk me away somewhere nice for a day trip, weekend or a holiday. She may ask where I'm going when I split. I always have something to do. I say I was going to go home, do some work, study, see a friend, meet my brother or sister, or go to the gym. Whatever I was going to do. Nothing she can come back to by saying "Okay, lets do that." On departing, I let her know that I had a nice enough time to consider another date (sometimes referring to particularly good new or improved Behaviour that took place) and enjoyed getting to know her more, in Reciprocation to her comments. I advise her to call me if she would like to speak or Invite me to come out with her again. Then it's back to square one. Incoming Calls. She needs to secure herself another Rendezvous with me if she wants one.

If there is something else I'd like her to do for me there and then, I tell her that I enjoyed her company and assumed we were departing, as she hasn't suggested anything. She is therefore prompted to suggest something or depart. She has to get in the mindset where she's asking me everything.

Rewarding Behaviour

*Be as sweet as the scratch, no sweeter,
and always stick a hoe for a
bundle before you sex her.*
Iceberg Slim

As long as a hoe is Choosing me, she can feel insecure about me, desire increased contact with me, more physical Intimacy, sex, any particular type of sex, to feel closer, to show me off socially, material things, ride in my car, see my home, holidays together, marriage. It doesn't matter what she wants. I don't need to fulfil her needs. Their absence mushrooms their value. Although it's imperative that I be fully aware of them as they are her motivation.

I compile what I call a "Wish List" in my head for each of my women. I omit desires that are against my principles, such as marriage, roses, lending money, putting my life story under a microscope, living together, marathon phone calls, visiting her, and having children. Anything that involves much expenditure or conceding the Balance of Power. Everyone is just slightly different and I need to know everyone's "wish list" of Intimacies, with the odd other specific Wish here and there. There is a standard blueprint of one in the next chapter. It's like a Christmas list, with things in order of most Wished for last. Wishes act as a kind of rocket fuel! I harness that energy by guiding the rocket in the right direction.

As I am aware of my hoe's List, and the importance of each Wish to her, I use them as a basis to Reward her for good Behaviour. I have to show my appreciation in the best way possible for her trying to conform to my Contract. Her motivation for this is her need to get me to Choose her so much that she obtains the Balance of Power - and can therefore stipulate and fulfil her own Wish and get me under her thumb. This is my rocket guidance system!

The Reward is always appropriate in value to her as her Behaviour was valuable to me, bearing in mind her

Potential. Potential is the formula that allows me to convert her Behaviour into the appropriate Reward. Evaluate whether she continues to receive the same Rewards, or she progresses. It's my exchange rate mechanism. If a woman uses one hundred percent of her Potential with me, she will receive the maximum Reward I can give to her at that point in time. It's not like every hoe that spends $50 gets X, spends $100, she gets Y. Einstein said that everything is relative.

Two hoes could each fly me business class to New York but it wouldn't mean they are both as sweet as each other. For one it might be something she had to save for months. So she's a Top Performer. The other could afford to buy me a car. So if I pulled out all the stops for that hoe, who has Potential, I'd have just told her that is all she needs to do to fulfil her wildest fantasies, when from her perspective she has not done much at all.

In other words, I'm only as sweet as she is. She will learn what gets her the results she Wishes. Just as we are all conditioned to go into autopilot, hit the nearest wall switch, and expect light, hoes are accustomed to using sex (or the mere hope of sex) to manipulate because it always worked for them. A mouse that's been used to one maze all its life will soon bump into dead ends in a new one. After it's bumped its nose against the wall a few times, it will quickly start to learn which new paths to the cheese are open. Take a left here, a right there...

So being understanding of me being in control, manners, effort, and such things as material and financial gains need to be Rewarded to encourage and show that I appreciate them. She will transfer to using generosity, good manners, consideration, unselfishness, money, and so on, if sex no longer works and the qualities I have just listed are enforced. Nothing is more natural to hoes than to manipulate, so it's not difficult.

Hoes don't impress me; they try to impress me.
Paradise

I act sweeter for a split second, to hint at the Reward, when a hoe says she will do something, but I always get my gift or Behaviour in advance. A favour for a favour. Not on credit. Nor can she negotiate or predetermine what she will get. When I am given clothes that I mentioned to her, DVD's I like, taken out somewhere nice, handed some gift vouchers or whatever, I exchange it for an appropriate Reward from her List. This will make her link cause with effect. It will be all the more poignant as I'll be keeping her at a level where she's always able to receive, and wishing for, more. My commodity is supreme, fascinating, desire. Not indulgence. Hoes prioritise money, tricks prioritise sex, a Fox prioritises being in control.

I don't deplete rocket fuel faster than it builds up, or I loose remote control and the rocket splutters and plummets down to earth. She doesn't get anything she Wishes unless I do. She leaps through the hoops. I throw her the odd crumb and she'll flip out! She'll savour it and appreciate it like nothing else. I don't break her off big chunks, then expect her to flip over crumbs again.

Pavlov's Dogs Theory: the named scientist trained dogs to salivate whenever they heard a bell. To condition them so as to obtain this result, he rang a bell prior to feeding them each mealtime.

It is imperative that a Reward is associated as directly as possible with the things I want to encourage, her taking care of us. The best way to do this is by immediately Rewarding her. I'm talking knee-jerk-reaction immediate, putting your foot down in a Murciélago immediate. This needs to be done consistently at first. This sequence is an unsaid thing. It's not declared or arranged between you both. Even if I could discuss it and agree upon it, it would not guarantee anything. I'm using the Laws of Reality, not "logical" reasoning and "logical" agreements, to ensure things go well. It's very simple: all that matters are her actions and my reactions.

When a hoe has just got my movie ticket, or we're leaving the restaurant on our first few dates, I might give her a blast of eye contact or I touch her arm lightly above the elbow as I smile and say thanks. Stand or sit closer to her than usual. Touch her in a way that could be almost accidental. Link her arm in mine. Quickly squeeze her hand. Briefly put her arm around me. Kiss her. Or simply kiss her cheek after she spoils me.

Mention her name. Or I might just say thanks, sexily, leaning real close to her ear. Or say nothing but do the same. If she has done something special according to her Potential, I show lots of appreciation, an appropriate special effort on my part too. Something highly enjoyable for her. The point is that it's not something I presume that she will enjoy from my perspective, but something I have made the effort to learn that she will enjoy. If her Potential is a lot higher, I'm not going thank her any more Intimately that I described above, until she makes a genuine effort.

When an Emotionally exciting object stimulates the subject simultaneously with one not Emotionally exciting, the latter may in time (often after one such joint stimulation) arouse the same Emotional reactions as the former.
John B Watson

Every time when something happens that is a big improvement or very considerate, I need to Reward it strongly by fulfilling a significant Wish on her List. But in certain circumstances it is impractical to do so instantly. You can only get so Intimate in public places without getting arrested! So I ensure that any time lapse between what she does and my Reward is minimal. The longer the time lapse, the more important it is that I immediately use some kind of promise to bridge the gap. A promise can be a verbal or physical indication. Anything from a nudge or touch to a whisper, as long as she understands it.

Visualise the brain as having well established highway that thoughts travel down, in order to arrive at desired objectives. Signs are necessary to point out the right direction. Soon enough she'll commission a brand new autobahn as it is confirmed as the easiest, the fastest and most scenic route to what she Wishes.

Intimacy

I don't try to make a girl's fantasy come true. I want
to be her fantasy. How can I be her fantasy
unless I allow her time to fantasise?
Paradise

As I highlighted in Front earlier, Sex and Emotion are inseparably intertwined. Sex consists of two elements: the physical and the psychological.

Two men could perform the exact same physical action with a woman, for example run their hand up her thigh. Man #1's hand might feel like it's radiating love and affection. Like white-hot magnesium lust searing along her nerves. Make her wetter than a monsoon, send chemicals rushing around her fast enough to split atoms, and blow her mind, as she thinks about and feels what's happening.

Whereas Man #2 doesn't even turn her on with the same light touch, an identical action. In fact she feels uncomfortable, doesn't trust him, thinks he's grotesque. It wouldn't matter what he did to her, her mind wouldn't be receptive. These opposite reactions are purely due to thought.

Now I'm not detracting from the importance of what one does, just emphasising that the mind is far more powerful. I mean it's so powerful that men and women can even come without physical stimulation! Take wet dreams, premature ejaculation or women coming at the thought of last night as examples of this.

You could fuck a girl who's been jocking you for a minute
for two hours, and you could fuck a girl that's been on
your nuts for a while for twenty minutes. I'll bet the
second broad will definitely get more out of it.
The Kidd

By the time a hoe is allowed to get really physical with me, she will have fantasised about it to the point of obsession. Her desire will have been baking for a long time, rising like dough in an oven. You've got to keep that heat on, not open the oven door to check, or reduce the temperature, or it'll sink. Keep it baking and eventually the crust will crack. Patience creates a lot of desire and therefore motivation. Curiosity kills hoe's cats! The longer we build up to aspirations, the better. And the slower we progress once we venture into this area the better. Everything will be amplified. It's record-breaking foreplay for her. Guinness should list me.

Intimacy is a principal way, but not the exclusive way, to Reward Behaviour, because a hoe's Wish List will consist principally of Intimacies, with the other desires dotted here and there. Things like going in my car, taking a photo, entering my house, and spending longer periods of time with me, hearing more about my life, talking about her favourite subjects, planning something, doing particular activities. I don't initiate contact through any other method than the one already established, unless it's to Reward her with one on the Wish list. The onus is on her to motivate the transition if she wants it.

From the first date, my woman can get more and more Intimate with me if she acts right. This happens on two levels. Instant, Temporary Intimacy is used for Rewarding Behaviour. Long-Term Intimacy is the general, every-day level of Intimacy we have between us.

Long-Term level of Intimacy is way, way behind the Temporary one, so that immediate Rewards always contrast against it. Long-term takes into account how we have got along over a period of time. It's our day-to-day default level of Intimacy. So, for instance, if she's Performed like a thoroughbred over the last few months, it will become normal to kiss me goodbye on the lips.

If I drew a graph illustrating the two levels of Intimacy, Temporary, to Reward Behaviour, would consist of quick, sharp peaks in a similar manner to those of a polygraph, whenever the hoe was sweet with me. Flatline in between. What she did for me last is yesterday's headline! Long-Term would show as a gradual, gentle line, shadowing the overall trend of those instant, Temporary peaks and dips.

Just like at Mc Donald's, you have to be doing well to earn those stars (Intimacies) one by one in order to be able to progress to the next. They're awarded, not taken.

Here's a rough outline of a Wish List from the point of view of Intimacy. It is not set in stone. In individual circumstances certain Wishes will be rearranged and of course a complete Wish List contains many other things, not only Intimacies, as I described earlier. Note how the majority can be classified as merely friendly behaviour.

*1   My company. Taking me out for up to a few hours.

*2   Expressions. Brief smiles.

*3   Entering her personal space or allowing her to enter mine for short periods.

*4   Light tactileness. Briefly, lightly, touching on the arm, back, hand.

*5   Brief eye-to-eye.

*6   Allowing her to briefly kiss my cheek.

*7   My company on all-day activities. Day trips.

*8   Allowing her to briefly link arms.

*9   Allowing her to briefly hug.

*10 Kissing her on the cheek.

*11 Briefly linking arms with her.

*12   Briefly hugging her.

*13   My company on overnight weekend breaks.

*14   Prolonged eye-to-eye.

*15   She may briefly kiss me on the lips.

*16   Allowing her to squeeze my hand, and hold briefly.

*17   Kissing her briefly on the lips.

*18   Squeezing her hand and holding briefly.

*19   Allowing her to give brief kisses.

*20   Allowing her to touch my upper body. Massage my feet or back.

*21   Lengthier, deeper kisses.

*22   My company on holidays.

And so on. It's all about recognising the value and controlling supply, and therefore influencing demand. Stars cannot be skipped. They have to be worked through, like you're not eligible to become a supervisor at Mc Donald's unless you have four Stars.

When a hoe does something that deserves *10, but she's currently only ever reached *2 because our relationship is new, we will progress to *3, and *4. That will be a significant way to show appreciation. Whereas if over time she had already worked her way up to *10, for that thing, she will get *10 again and again, each time she does that thing for us. I am only going to indulge bigger Wishes when something improves.

You can have hoes for years that have yet to get some "urban legend." Some may never do. One can't be a Fox without control. I'm getting what I want because of what she Wishes for, not what she gets. It is too true that in life happiness is in the journey, it's not a destination.

If you could eat your dream meal every day, how would you then feel about it? Imagine how you would feel being accepted for a job after training for a year, filling in an eight page application, enduring four days of tests, interviews and practical assessments - and then how you'd conduct yourself whilst on a probationary one day contract.

Hoes will always try and get what they want. When we go out, it's often apparent girls are itching to hug or kiss. Sometimes their arms move slightly. If I'm not ready to get Intimate, she hasn't done anything for me yet except turn up. I greet her stood at a slight distance. I don't face her with my body too, if I feel that the distance alone is insufficient to refrain her. And so with a firm commitment and thoughtful conduct I can usually avoid being taken advantage of, or becoming treated like an instant mouldable boyfriend, without saying a thing.

Kissing a hoe on the first or second date is inconceivable. My mere presence is Reward enough. Remember how I told you what brings fronting to a conclusion? Hoes often front all evening, then suddenly pounce right at the end of the night, when they get desperate as we say goodbye. If it's not deserved yet, I transform it into a quick air peck with an evasive manoeuvre, as they home in on my lips. Air kiss her cheek.

It can occasionally happen that after some instant Intimacy, a hoe will assume that she's gained control. She may mistake a temporary Reward as a new Long-Term level of Intimacy. I don't let her get all tactile with me all of a sudden after a little Intimacy has taken place. It's DON'T TOUCH like wet paint! Should she Wish to hold my hand in the street, rest her leg against mine under the table, kiss me, or cuddle impromptu, she'll get nowhere, unless Long-Term Intimacy allows it. When her hands start roaming too far as we kiss, I check her instantly. I gently ease her hand back somewhere tamer, hold her hand, or to really get her curious, ice the whole thing. So I clearly define our boundaries.

Females do this often when they are in Power and their Wishes are not being satisfied. They are very good at it. So most males, or their friends, will have numerous examples of their advances being rejected or restricted that they can look on as a free demonstration. Because if you are male, it initially takes some learning and confidence to step out of the Matrix.

If we've reached a stage where she's doing great consistently, our Long-Term level will have risen accordingly. When we depart she might be able to get her arms around me for a second, should she grab my hand over the dinner table, I'll squeeze hers for a few seconds before releasing it. She can lean against me, or I let her embrace me for a long moment before cutting her loose.

In any scenario, I have some vocab. on cue. My favourites go something like, "I know we kissed the last time we saw each other. But that was then. It felt right, but right now I feel like getting to know you more."

"We will always be friends more than we are anything else. I put that first and foremost. Nothing is more important."

"I'm only just getting to know you."

"I was comfortable with what we were doing."

"Don't take me for granted."

"Let's take our time and really get to know each other. I'm not easily tactile with people, but when I am it means more than someone who is all the time with everyone."

"Let's not rush. I want to feel right. Let's let things develop naturally. Give me a little time."

"This isn't the right time or place." To hint at better Rendezvous. It's like I'm parodying classic bitch Behaviour! Check out some of those stereotypical "guy coming on to girl" scenes in the movies!

Desire is the very essence of man.
Baruch Spinoza

120

The Law of Reciprocation II

Get lots, give a little, then get lots more.
The Kidd

It is now relevant to explain how the Law of Reciprocation applies to my relationships. I shall say this once only and only once. There's virtually no Reciprocation when it comes to the queen's faces. Instead, I Reward with anything else from the Wish list.

I pay as close to zero percent of all expenses as possible. When a hoe is with me, she gets the company of a handsome, immaculate, fun, sexy, happy, intelligent, lavish, deep, sensitive, Powerful, ambitious, consistent, sincere, caring man with principles, who is like no other on the planet. So I may be in danger of being over confident, although I do not wish to be, but I certainly am not in any danger of being insecure and getting exploited because of it.

I am able to give something priceless: my time. I'm the only one who has it to give. So she doesn't really care if I don't try to buy her affection like a trick does. So when I am not looked upon as a trick to be manipulated, or at least one to be manipulated in the short term with basic manipulation, the way I Reciprocate is very desirable. They can deal with tricks any old time to indulge themselves in their usual games. Whereas they have to treat me with respect, and that can be very attractive.

Some men foolishly believe that if a woman volunteers to pay or split bills, makes a reasonable effort, and acts as a genuine friend, she can't be a hoe, she must have honourable, pure, intentions. That she has passed some kind of definitive test. If this happens frequently, without any kind of counter manipulation on the man's side, then she may be genuine. But it also may that she is more sophisticated at manipulation than average. There is an old con, or sales technique, where the idea is to get three yeses. The first two are genuine and therefore guaranteed not to fail, so long as the victim is listening or interacting. They set you up for the third yes, which is the stinger. You are more likely to fall for the stinger because you have witnessed their goodness by doing several good deeds for you, so you feel trust and obligation. Or they get you to agree on two points, comforting you, approving you, opening you up to be positive on the third. Just like a turkey gets fed before Christmas.

Look through the newspapers and see all these people who get divorces and take half, or so, of their husband or wife's money. Look at your friends who have debt because their partner has ran it up. Observe those people who significantly gain from moving in with the other.

Deception is a hoe weapon. She's not perturbed about spending chips, she's playing for the big jackpot. What does spending ten grand matter to her if it wins a gold-digger-conscious businessman over, and he then buys her whatever she Wishes, then marries her?

So whilst I do not discriminate against a genuine person who treats me with equal respect and care, I do not consider being given a plate of food or several plates of food, proof of that.

The only money I have spent with any of my current Top Performers is the cost of gas for me to travel to Rendezvous. I may occasionally take care of something small. It's no big deal, but it must be insignificant in relation to their generosity with me. This simple formula allows me to gauge what's appropriate. Things like shall I buy aperitifs whilst she's in the cloakroom could be circumnavigated by establishing a tab. But there may be times in established relationships when I'm asked for a small favour. She's out of change, do I have any for the parking meter? The answer is easy, yes.

Unless in an exclusive and serious relationship that has gone well past the dating stage, I give nothing for Valentine's Day. I'm not seeking anyone's affections. Friends or people who date don't send each other Valentine cards. She can send me one and give me a present if she feels the inclination. If I'm single, dating, I'm busy on Valentine's day, birthdays and at Christmas.

122

Hoes can take me out on a different day - let them wonder.

Long established Top Performers may simply receive a birthday, Christmas or get well card, as from any friend. It'll be friendly or fun. Nothing romantic. Later on, when we are high enough up the Long-Term Intimacies, it is possible to get (relatively) small gifts. They shouldn't relate to activities both of us can participate in, unless it's equipment or a restaurant, cooking, activity or travel guide book. So no theatre tickets, weekend breaks, hotel stays. Or I buy something that will be of interest to her.

When my women pay me compliments, I receive them with the slight indifference of someone who doesn't believe them and has heard it before, yet with a touch of appreciation for her openness. I rather she show that she likes me than just talk about it. I say thanks, or nothing, and carry on. Or I use the opportunity to communicate that I feel actions speak louder. "That's nice of you to say. I'm not sure though. I suppose it's hard to believe, but when you [highlight something she does that I appreciate] I kind of believe what you say to me." Or harder, "My sentimental side wants to believe you, but then why don't you show me by..."

The best time for me to give out compliments is to Reward Behaviour. They are compliments she Wishes to hear. They are also about things I that I wish to encourage. The best things she has done for me, the things I most appreciate. Giving just one at a time means it gets considered more and means more.

I will remark that I thought it was sweet the other day when she asked me if I wanted an ice cream as we passed a shop. It was thoughtful of her to ask me where I'd like to go this autumn. I felt closer to her when she took me skiing. I had fun with her when she took me to the Oriental in Bangkok. It was special when we dined at Jules Verne's. I like that she is intelligent, independent, and has initiative. A woman without initiative is the biggest turnoff to me. I like that she plans things. She is so thoughtful with me when she gets me things I have mentioned. That each time she does these things it tells me that she's my friend so she never need say anything to me.

I only compliment regarding her appearance if she specifically asks me for my opinion. When I do so, I don't get carried away. My comments are not sexually charged. She looks smart. Takes good care of her hair. That she applies her makeup well and varies her style. She has taste in her clothes and colour schemes. Her nails are nicely manicured. She has a nice smile. Nice eyes. She seems to have good standards of hygiene. I do not want to distract her focus too much from how she treats me, because she will naturally take good care of her appearance anyway.

Only when I'm specifically asked what's sexy on her, if her ass is too fat or if she should loose some weight, if her hair could be neater, if I like the makeup colours, do I talk about it. I politely, considerately, tell her the truth.

I also say I like them for how they are, not what they are. I also tell her that it's a matter of personal opinion and hers is the one that counts more than mine or anyone else's. As it's her body, she should feel happy with herself rather than rely on others to feel good. I understand that women instinctively try to improve their looks to gain the Balance of Power anyway, so I leave this to her.

A girl can be insistent to know what I least like, physically, about her. So although I will usually instead point out one specific improvement in manners, in being considerate, in generosity, sometimes a physical observation is insisted upon. I choose one thing only, that she could improve. "Sometimes your hair doesn't look as smart as others. Your nails would look more elegant if they were neater; there are some occasions when you could apply your makeup with more care. You occasionally look tired so you should get more sleep. I think blue jeans are very common. I was surprised to see your shoes were a little scuffed. Your grammar is sometimes incorrect. I think you should floss a little more regularly."

If asked for more than one point I say that I will have to think about it and tell her later. I never make more than one point per occasion.

When being Intimate, I initiate things, or give signs of encouragement. After that happens, then I reciprocate as little as possible as I take things forward, or let her move things forward. So, for example, I might kiss her for a few seconds, but from then on it's her tongue in my mouth, she's kissing me, as I lean gently backwards to encourage her, she's leaning towards me or over to me. My clothes don't come off unless they're taken off. She undresses me like Toshiro Mifune in Red Sun. It means sex is not all me on top, me doing all the work. She gets over me, she makes a lot of effort too. I'm seductively "lazy" - a hoe trips off what she can do to me as well as what I do to her. There are many women who go their whole lives never even knowing how to have sex, because they relinquish it to men. And there are plenty of men plugged into the Matrix living out a fantasy that they are some strong conqueror because they make all the effort in a relationship, including in bed. This is why fake orgasms exist. It's gratifying for men to massage their ego with this perception because the other option is to admit they are conquered and working hard for the female in many areas, due to their sexual impatience.

Wealth Front & Clout

If a cat hits on his rib for a grand, and he ain't got nothing worth a grand, the bitch can tell him he couldn't need it, he just wanted it. But if a cat pulled up sharp, wearing ice & driving a new Cadillac, he could need a G for a number of things, because he'd represent thirty G without saying a word.
Andrew Stonewall Jackson

It's not polite to ask someone how much they earn or to be seen openly calculating their net worth unless you are very familiar with, and trusted by, the other person. And even so, it can raise suspicion. And rightly so, because what use is it to anyone except a hoe who prioritises financial gain at another's expense? There are a few people interested in learning about business and success purely to improve their own efforts though. The latter are highly likely to explain their motives and make them clear by their actions.

Despite this, some hoes are so accustomed to having the Balance of Power that they like to flaunt it and will ask blatantly, when they first meet someone, about their financial situation. Some hoes even have the audacity to enquire how much money I make. I take it like this: just think when she's on my team! She knows it's out of order, bad etiquette. She can evidently see if I'm broke or not. I answer in an appropriately uninformative manner to let her know I'm not a trick, such as, "Well I'm from almost nothing to almost something." Or, "Enough for the lifestyle that I have, not enough for the lifestyle that I would like." Or, "I'm more concerned about your financial situation actually, so give me some details! You're not in debt are you?" Or ignore her question with an icy silence, and continue talking as normal, as if it never happened.

I use a hoe's fascination with my Wealth Front and Clout as an opener to cut into her ambitious side if she has less Clout. Then advise her, if she will take notice.

Email: Thanks for your mail. So, really being nosey now, how much money do you make? How much rent do you pay? Give me some figures!!! I wanna know. Cos you drive around in an expensive car, not like my Ford. Or are you one of these people who as soon as they get their money they spend it on cars and CDs and things? I'll write maybe later or tomorrow, ok.

"Is that watch real?"

"Yeah, the hands go around and everything."

When somebody remarks about Wealth Front or Clout I thank them genuinely, frankly and casually. I don't make a conversation of it unless they do. It's only an object. If they ask how much an item was, I state that I don't recall, I have owned it quite a while.

Someone was asking me if I carry a large bankroll on me for hoes to admire. I'm a 21st Century Fox; my women are more likely to see a cross-eyed, albino dodo flying through the sky than ever see me reach into my pocket. But there are rare occasions when I buy myself things when with hoes. However, if I was out and about solo, cashiers and onlookers would spot a roll. In my opinion, an ostentatious, perhaps suspicious, wad of money is the wrong way to strengthen my Front, because it can look contrived and low-class. Only Low Clout hoes will be affected in the right way by the sight of waddage and they'll start showing me more interest than my ISA, asking questions like they're a quiz show host.

My personal preference is to use my platinum or charity cards. They communicate more than a fat bankroll will do to most people. Till tappers dig the platinum. I carry what is most useful and advantageous to me. I don't do anything to impress hoes, further than being myself.

The more Clout I have, and the more I behave like a Fox, the easier a hoe gets into the mindset that she's got to prove her self. I'm solvent. If I'm refusing to pay for something, or checking her on something, a hoe can invariably see that it's my principles and feelings that are the issue, rather than money being a problem.

128

I never go for the, "I can't afford to" angle. Players and tricks ask hoes for sympathy. Hoes ask Foxes what they can do for them.

Money attracts money in other ways too. Stinking Front and Clout demonstrates to hoes that I am competent at attaining and advising on financial matters. Therefore hoes are more likely to seek and consider my advice on their own situations.

Hoe's egos love successful people or people with evident Potential. The larger you are, the more money you go through. A wino with a grand would consider himself as having a cash surplus available to spend. A hoe would easily be able to see I can eat up over a grand on clothes like that. That my car costs to run. I go to a golf and health club. Foreign and domestic travel. All sorts. My lifestyle consumes a lot of waddage. I prioritise saving and investing too, so I'm financially sound and worry free in the future. If I did have debts, then of course I'd prioritise paying them off.

I am open about the above priorities. But I do not want to detract from my highest priority: how I'm treated. I'm sensitive to how people are with me. I like good manners, I like to be spoilt and I like doers not talkers. So I need to give hoes opportunity to be sweet and express their character rather than deny them it by charging ahead like the aforementioned deluded conqueror. This maintains my Clout whilst it encourages hoes to be sweet.

Wait Training

Pristine desire is forged in the crucible of torture.
The purest joy is in great anxiety relieved.
Trick Baby, by Iceberg Slim

Hoes will try to run things at their pace. I took my first countermeasure in my Contract, by communicating that I lead a busy lifestyle. In this chapter I'm going deeper into how I lead my life at my pace and use my time as I please whilst managing a large stable, or having one exclusive relationship.

I determine the value of my time by making it scarce. Therefore I can add it to the Wish list. If you value yourself and your time, others have to do too. And so a side effect of Wait Training is about being patient enough to ensure that every time a hoe Wishes for something, she has to Wait that little longer so her Power will be drained like a bathtub and I will be on her mind even more. And that's where I want to be. Anticipation is over half of pleasure. It makes it more special.

As a rule of thumb, unless I have a full stable, no matter how many women are involved with me, I plan my time with my hoes as if I'm dealing with many more. I allow for my personal free time as well. This means that my current stable don't restrict my time, or opportunities to make new Copps. I'm fair, honest and consistent with my hoes from day one. When my stable grows or diminishes, it has no effect on my current relationships. I never have a Miss I-See-You-Every-Few-Days suddenly wondering what's happened and I won't be answering phone calls and texts every two minutes! None of my hoes have Wait problems. I go on holiday when I please, they can Wait until I'm back. Oh, but they *can't* Wait!

It's also good for it to be understand that I'm not a doctor. I'm not on call. They cannot ring me up to arrange an impromptu meeting later that night, or the following day. Good things come to those who Wait. I allow a hoe time to wonder what I'm doing in the meantime, why I'm not rushing over to see her before she's hung up, to think about our date and me, time for her mind to fantasise. How can I be a hoe's fantasy unless I allow her time to fantasise? This is how I can be taking her to the "final frontier" whilst she's taking me to Athens!

How are Direct Debits advertised? "Don't worry - it's taken care of!" This is not the way to have a vibrant relationship with someone who can be manipulative. I keep the frequency of all Rendezvous irregular. I take bookings one at a time. I don't entertain arrangements to Rendezvous repeatedly on set days. I prefer to know that I'm desired and that she is wanting to meet, each time we meet. It's much healthier than a regular obligation to fulfil on her, or my, side. It's good for the Balance of Power too.

I allow a Rendezvous usually once a fortnight, occasionally once a week, if they're requesting dates that often. Another way to manage my time, status and long-term expectations well is to meet a little later than hoes want. Every so often she will find out that I can't meet on the date she wishes, due to a prior commitment. This will be anything from seeing a friend, a date, shopping, family occasion, party, gym, to free time to myself. It doesn't have to sound important. I'm being honest about things. My life's so full that it is increasingly necessary for me to fit normally trivial activities in.

I will be busy doing things most of the time, so hoes can't expect to dial my number and hear my voice whenever they get the inclination. Most unscheduled calls go unanswered because I'm busy. Otherwise I'll be encouraging interruptions for myself and setting up disappointment for her in future. Of course I have voicemail and I check my messages, emails and texts, returning them at my own pace. Whichever method of communication I wish to encourage more I give more priority to. Ninety-nine percent of connected voice calls to me are arranged in advance, out of courtesy, to ensure that I'm free. This allows a hoe to communicate with me and for me to stay at the forefront of her mind. Especially since she knows I always reply, but never when I will. My telephone has no power over me, I always teach a hoe from the outset that I will respond to her in my own time when she contacts me, and to bear with me if she doesn't receive an immediate reply, but she will always get one.

A fast response for me is same day. Normal is during the following day or two. But this is not some rigid plan and the little touch of randomness from this relaxed attitude is very exciting and unpredictable. Qualities that are attributes to any relationship as I will discuss in Advanced Rewarding.

If tested about my laid-back communication style, I'll explain, "I like to give whatever I'm doing my full, undivided attention. I don't enjoy feeling rushed, or my mind being distracted. That's how I can be so busy, yet still enjoy my life. When I'm working hard, or studying, or out with people, including you, I don't use my mobile. So just like I might be busy when you text me, when I do respond to you, I will be focused on replying to you and thinking about what you wrote to me." I never reply straight away. I set the standards. We move at my pace. She soon understands that I'm a busy person and that she must fit into my life.

Email: I'm sorry but I'm gonna have to send you this, I just can't stop myself. I would love to talk to you on the phone but I'm scared to in a way. Would you like to talk on the phone with me? Maybe you're thinking "This girl's blowing this whole email and chat thing out of proportion, she's making this out to be something that it simply isn't." Well I guess you'd be right but because it's the most enormous tease it's like it's built something up inside me so big now yet I can't actually have it. It's not quite real, and here I am again, thinking about you a lot today and just can't find the discipline to leave you alone for one night. So sorry. I'm not the sort of person at all who doesn't give anyone breathing space, honestly, so please don't worry. It's just that chatting and emailing you is the next best thing to "being" with you, and right now I just can't get enough of it. So there you have it, a self confessed [Paradise] seeker! I'm actually surprised at myself for wanting this so much. You know that I could talk to you again all evening tonight don't you, or tomorrow or the next day! Ah well. Good thoughts though.

Evidence II

I don't worry about my women.
They worry about me.
Unknown

Each hoe's actions tell her story. I totally disregard what she says unless it correlates to what comes out of her actions or purse. I will know her inside out. I'll recognise changes in her Behaviour and in the amount of fronting and testing that takes place. These are logical extension of those in my first essay, so I shall be brief.

There is a cause for every effect. Night-time and weekend emails, voicemail and texts mean a hoe isn't getting much action as well as committing prime time to communicate with me.

Jealous behaviour is positive Evidence, keeping a hoe's mind occupied, acting like a swamp foundation on which she can't build her Power, and promoting competitiveness. Excessive jealousy means she hasn't got her orientation with regards to expectations, she needs more consistent Wait Training and better communication of the Contract.

Alterations in appearance or conduct further down the line are good Power barometers too. Should they start rationing the makeup, stop smelling like a French whore, wear more casual attire, turn up on time for dates (instead of early) or stop crying when we split, I would know that they are Choosing me less. Perhaps they are feeling more secure, or if we are single, they have something else interesting going on.

Good indications of the Balance of Power include seeing something I've informed a girl will look stylish or something I don't like result in action. When hoes speak of looking through our older emails, keeping our cinema tickets, storing my text messages for months or use "we" and futuristic references.

One-word or one-sentence answers when we're talking signal impending testing, unless she's reacting like that because I'm blowing her mind with something I'm saying.

A decrease in her frequency of contact with me indicates that she is Choosing me less, or it could be a test. There is often likely to be a new trick on the scene, a new female friend, or she will be feeling she has too slim a chance of being my woman. This is covered in "Bolting."

My reader, I have never seen anyone in a movie as talented at acting as some of these hoes, believe me, I would nominate 'em anytime. They make Marlon Brando look like an amateur. Although I never trust anyone one hundred percent (I only trust myself ninety-nine percent) I trust hoes to a degree. The only thing you can trust her on hundred percent on is that she will be a hoe. Nowadays I find it a cinch to know when a hoe is bullshitting me. I have ESP. But this comes with observation and experience. To elaborate on it would consume half of this book. What I can do is build upon the above Evidence and tell you a few basic methods that help me pick up on vibes.

One is if a hoe's lips are moving. Naw, seriously, the main one I use is something that can be observed at any time. When we access different parts of our brain, our eyes instinctively look in certain directions. One way when we recall information from memory. Another when we use our mind creatively to invent, to imagine, to tell tales. In case the subject has pre-prepared a cover, which will be recalled, it's necessary to ask unexpected questions.

To use this technique, I suggest observing and noting someone's eyes during conversation. First ask them a few questions about, or observe them talking about, easily recalled facts. Then watch as you tentatively try them on something that will require invention. You can even select the cast interviews on one of your DVD's, sit back and observe.

Packaging

It's like a game of chess. You
must think first, before you move.
Unknown

"Packaging" is how I communicate, both verbally and by my actions. A Fox must be great communicator. Hoes are looking for quite different messages than those that I wish to communicate to them: it is possible for Intimacy, honesty, privacy, patience, and respect to be interpreted as weakness, fear, and conformity to their needs, because they are so keen have, and accustomed to having, the Balance of Power. So I devise my actions carefully so that they aren't misinterpreted. I have to be considerate to ensure that my actions and words are understood.

My principles are steadfast, I don't change myself for anyone, but I do adapt my communication. I Package my words and actions so that they are expertly tailored to their particular recipient and the circumstance.

Unless it's justified as I explained in Rewarding, I kill all flirting. It leaves you with about as much Power as an eastern European car. I'm the one saying, "Don't call me babe, call me by my name." Sitting in a booth in a nightclub, a friend of a friend of a friend suddenly walked up and slid onto my lap. Her hand resting right next to the kingsiza. She had never even spoken to me before. Without a motion, I said commandingly but warmly into her ear, "Look, I don't know you, but if you want to get to know me, get up, sit next to me and we will talk." I also handle strangers' requests for drinks diplomatically. "Who do you think you're talking to? Go and get some guy to buy you a drink, then, if that's not all you're about, if you can guarantee me decent conversation, come back here." I could get her to hoe a drink for me too. I can also interact and Package more by asking her in the middle of it, "Do you know what the most expensive drinks they sell here are?" And, "I bet you can't get bought a [insert expensive or amusing drink name] as a fun challenge.

When a hoe says "I missed you, did you miss me?" I reply that I haven't had much chance to think, I've been rather busy, I try to focus on what I'm doing, like I am on us now. It's nice to be out with her in this restaurant now. Or yes, I thought of her yesterday when I put on the shirt she gave me. This Packages to her what she might do to impress me the most. She is only guaranteed my attention when she's with me.

Should hoes discuss us doing something in the future, and it's still early days, I insert the following phrases into my replies. "Let's talk about that next time." Or, "If we are still friends..." Or, "If I get to know you better..." Or," If we continue to get along like we are doing..." This way it's understood they haven't got the Balance of Power, understand that our relationship is not on autopilot and are more motivated.

I don't leave items of mine in my hoe's vehicles, allow them to lend me things or leave articles behind at my house. Those little things convey a sense of entitlement or assurance of approval. I try to keep egos as down to earth as possible.

The fact that when I'm single I don't disclose intimate details about other women I date may be mistaken for fear of disapproval. Privacy may be mistook as hiding something, which I am certainly not. So I want to be sure that it's understood that I regard anything that I do (or don't do) sexually, or anyone does sexually with me, as confidential. It's not something I gossip to others about. I'm upfront and open about the fact that I go on dates when I'm single, but just not the Intimate details. Hoes should respect my discretion. It also applies to them. A Real Man or woman is respected because of their integrity and that they can be trusted regarding all private matters, including Intimacy.

Another wrong impression can be taken from the fact that I often don't carry my mobile with me, or I silence it when I'm out on dates. So I have to ensure that I communicate that this is because I don't want to be interrupted when I'm busy. This can be Packaged through general conversation, or explained if asked about it. Or I might advise her to consider doing the same.

Next we come to honesty. Hoes will, by nature, lie and front. It's what first-class hoes do. It's no stress to me. And why shouldn't they test to see if I'm the real McCoy in this imperfect world in which we live? I don't let a hoe know every time she lies to me. I decide in each individual case. For example, if we are single and dating, or just good friends, there may be no point telling a hoe that she is lying about dating with someone else to try and make me jealous. She will interpret it as jealousy. I'll respond to her as if she was telling the truth: I'll tell her I'm happy for her, or not do anything at all. But if it is not to my detriment, I Fire a hoe who has lied to me about things that are directly connected with me. For example, if she was supposed to do something for me and lied about it.

I care only how she is with me. I don't care what my hoes do and how they are with other people in terms of integrity and respect. And I would go crazy trying to figure all of that out too. It's their business. I don't need to know everything my hoe has done, with whom and when, since she last met me. Requesting much detail without her volunteering it can broadcast the wrong signals. A hoe will open up to me as far as she feels comfortable doing. It's my job to know what's going on in my women's minds, not their soap opera worlds.

Hoes will occasionally volunteer anecdotes about dates with male friends. It's an attempt to obtain Power. Whether they are lying or honest, my reaction is the same. I'll tell them, "Have a really nice night. Have a cool - or even hot - time!" It obliterates their Power, shows I'm a good friend and demonstrates my integrity.

If I am single and hoes enquire about my friends or dates, however nosy they want to be about my female friends, I will tell it like it is. She might ask if I've had sex with any of them. I'll reply something along the lines of "I'm single and if I'm intimate with anyone or not is my own business, thank you." Or tell her she needs to know me better to be asking me those kind of private questions. Now she can act how she wants, go silent, get upset, turn on the waterworks, pretend she's cool and talk about other guys to me, whatever. She knew from day one that I date and have female friends. She knows she is not my wife or girlfriend. It's all a fronting game to deduce if she's got any Power. When she realises that she's not able to manipulate me, she'll stop. She'll get no reaction. In fact she'll get the opposite. I might display mild doubt that she's eligible for me. There's no way I'm going to make her feel secure enough to start to lay down her own Contract with me and start doing what she orders. Friends don't do that. We're friends and if she stepped over that line, I didn't ask her to. I could say, "I'm fine to answer anything. Honesty is important to me. Remember it's you asking me the questions. I thought we were getting along, becoming good friends, but friends don't act like this. Sex isn't evil, I don't like people who have problems with sex. When a friend of mine is happy I feel good for them that they are." I do this in the tone that they are sounding incompatible as my friend. In my experience, within minutes the hoe is back to her old self again, flirting, chatting, and asking me out. If not she can go home or race me to hang up the phone and call back when she's composed herself and wants to treat me with respect.

As a follow up to any sex Power games, when the hoe next starts to make a move on me, I recoil or freeze her just as she's closing in on my lips. I'll say something along the lines of, "I know how you were the other day, you said you felt bad. I don't want our friendship to be damaged. I don't want unhappy people around me." No prizes for guessing the next words to escape her mouth in response. This prompts her to acknowledge in no uncertain terms that she accepts my Contract. It bumps up my Power. It enforces the fact that although the transition from friends to friends who kiss has taken place, it is simply that. She cannot mistake it for a transition of Power, or the start of a boyfriend and girlfriend relationship. It's duck's ass tight.

The decision to be single and only date casually, or to have an exclusive boyfriend and girlfriend type of relationship needs to be clearly understood and that must come from a clear mind on my part. A Fox can't be confused or unsure, or else it will manifest in some manner and cause problems.

140

Packaging is how information is presented. Like giving a gift in a nice wrapping with a huge neat bow will delight someone just as much as the contents, or messy paper and a scuffed box will make the item inside look bad. I am as direct in my response to challenges or questions as they are to me. Otherwise, everything is indirect, wrapped in cotton wool. I send my Package across to her extremely tacitly. Let's say I might be thinking that she's testing for the Balance of Power, she's desperate to get some "urban legend," she's immature, or that she's lying about her sex life or Clout. I don't say so. *Disclosing* my own understanding of this manipulation brings no advantage. Telling your opponent you understand their tactics is foolish. A situation of accusal and denial can ensue. It changes the focus onto more unworthy areas. It pollutes the information pool. Hoes also see if they can draw sympathy from people with their superb thespian skills by feigning fear, being upset, or with crocodile tears. They get no encouragement. No Reward. If she ever drags it up I put her on the defence, telling her how she spoilt the evening and she was too absorbed in herself. If she had the waterworks turned on because I tested out on something, I highlight that she wasn't listening to me and because of that fact, she had upset herself and that distanced her from me. She turned me off her. What about how I felt when she acted like that?

However if there is some reasonable external reason for my girl to be upset, I'm there for her to talk to and lean on. I empathise if warranted, but I never sympathise.

Offence is the best defence.
Paradise

When some sort of checking takes place on her or my part, it is necessary to be aware of who is on the offensive and who is on the defensive. The latter stance is never successful and is used only by the party lacking Power. I don't initiate confrontation, because from day one things are always as I desire, and I'm never defensive when tested. I put the spotlight on her character, highlight my Contract, talk about my feelings, what I think and what I want.

Once one is aware that a hoe is always trying to make herself the centre of conversation it is very simple to avoid Reciprocating self-centred remarks and make the conversation so that she must defend herself and concede. As I have said elsewhere: swift checking is effective, prolonged conversation is not.

Testing takes many forms. If a hoe doesn't call me when she says so, I don't waste my time reacting or giving myself a problem. I don't chump off my time making calls. I have free time to utilise. I'm seriously laid back like the Malibu adverts. If she contacts me in future, and if she asks, she will be advised I didn't mind that we didn't speak. I just carried on with my life, went out and had a good time, but I did mind that she didn't take seriously the necessity to keep her word with me. She'll get checked like an abandoned car outside the UN, but I'll be very calm and suave about it; I don't want to display (or experience) anger. That would convey Emotional Dependency.

Top Performance

There are only two reasons why a beggar begs. Firstly,
they know it gets results. The other reason is even
more important. They are so desperate to receive,
that they adopt a "by any means necessary" mode so
their vanity, their fronting, is conquered by desire.
This is enabled by scarcity.
Paradise

Once I have already established that the nicer hoes are
with me, the nicer I am with them, and things are going
well, it's possible to consider how good things can get.
My expectations should be reasonable, and based on
considerate understanding, as I outlined in Potential. Top
Performance means having the best relationship,
reaching that full Potential. Virtually everything you have
read up to this point creates the necessary climate for
this. So it can naturally evolve and improve over time. It
is my responsibility to Reward Behaviour, encourage it
positively and not dampen it with impatience, moods,
anger, greed, or any negative or forceful conduct.

I never ask a hoe for anything unless I have absolute
Power, am prompted to by her, or if I'm declining an
Rendezvous offer by giving an alternative suggestion.

My immediate reaction to, and appreciation of, being
bought popcorn at the cinema will encourage a hoe to
offer me Ben n' Jerry's next, to which my reaction will
make her more likely to get me the DVD I'm looking at
in the foyer of a store afterwards. It encourages her to
buy me popcorn next time, so it will become a standard
thing to then improve on. The generosity and respect
gradually builds up like rolling a snowball, then
avalanches.

When she does nothing, I do nothing. No reaction to
leave a negative memory or impression of me that
reduces her desire to be around me.

I don't worry about Top Performance, they should.
However, to do the best I can on my part to help, and

not hinder, good things from happening I employ some additional logic. I have already described Firing, used if a hoe goes one step further and tries to get me to do something, or breaches her Contract. Now I will set out some other methods for you.

I have to be good at communicating, allow hoes to understand my desires and what makes me happy so that they can focus on the right things. There's no point receiving a bottle of red wine if I like white wine; getting kisses in one place which is less preferable to another; or being taken to an Italian restaurant if I don't like pizza and pasta; or being given an expensive bag that I dislike. Whilst early on it is petty to be concerned with these details and it is important to Reward and appreciate the fundamental generosity, later I must take responsibility for effectively communicating my preferences.

Improvements and preferences are suggested by references to items I want during conversations, waking past a store window and showing an interest, criticising something I already have and saying I will replace it with something specific. I can mention that I like something my friend has, or that she has, and specify why I like it.

Sometimes hoes recognise their stable mate's realisation of their own Wishes and duplicate their actions to obtain similar results. I must be requested for this information. But that is not a problem since a hoe's insecurity will compel her to enquire if my recent holiday or night in watching movies with a take-away was in female company.

Holidays and short breaks even to the most discerning venues are not difficult objectives because being in my company for prolonged periods of time will naturally be high up a hoe's Wish list, as I explained in Wait Training. So some cases of apparent generosity are not as generous and as others. Of course, the more consideration of my preferences the more generous she is being. Consideration for me can be encouraged by me asking questions before accepting an invitation: what kind of place is it, and does it have specific things that I want. Or by asking them if they considered a different place.

Later on in Low to Medium Clout relationships, having a gift to bring might be a good excuse for someone to visit me at home. Some hoes will get into the routine of calling me when they have something for me. I'll say she can bring it over. I might let her explore new rooms because she's getting me furnishings for them. As you can imagine, getting bedroom accessories isn't difficult.

One method of starting a helpful routine is not to ask her to buy me something, but to collect something for me. With a Low Clouter, I'd tell her, "On your way over, stop at the [store] - I need some [any items from a DVD to a takeaway or groceries, to my dry cleaning.]" Something that I would buy anyway. If she quibbles, I can say we'll have to cancel or substantially delay her visit because I'll need to go out, or Fire-blast her on the phone - after all, I'm being hospitable to her; it's the least she can do.

When she arrives and hands over the goodies, I give her a tiny Reward for collecting. If she tries to hand me the receipt, I give her a "foxtrot oscar" look. I tell her to put it in the trash. Even if she wants paying, she can tell me the figure: I'm not going to be handed a receipt. If she asks me to, I pay her. She's saved me a trip, I still win. I can repeat the exercise and perhaps in future she'll be more giving. If she doesn't comment about the bill, I wait for a length of time to elapse, and create a psychologically Powerful situation, perhaps hand her a drink, or tell her to help herself, as I say, when close to her, "That was sweet of you to bring me the shopping. Were you wanting some money for it?/How much do I owe you for it?" If she tells me not to mind I Reward her. After a repetition I'll dump the, "I offer to pay and she declines" routine. I'll just receive and show my appreciation.

It is possible that the first time a hoe mentions purchasing me something material will be at a traditional gift giving time. I want a woman to be sweet with me all year round, so when a hoe mentions my present prior to my birthday or Christmas, I transform this annual event into a three hundred and sixty-five day a year open season. "I'd rather you didn't buy me anything for my birthday, feel pressure because of the time of year, or because society tells you to. I would prefer that you just

145

gave me something when you feel you want to. I'd rather you get me something because you're caring, and your thoughts are behind it, not because of a number on a calendar. You say you want to do it because you want to show I mean something to you. Well it will mean more to me because of your thoughtfulness." Done. It also can be useful to mention that I love surprises, and this can also be stated on occasions when I give her surprises outside of society's standard gift giving times.

Foxes never reject any gift on any day of the year. Not because of the quantity, the cost, my Wishes, or to prat. Not for any reason.

You may be wondering why this varies from my Invite rejection principle? Because seeing me is a necessity to her (*1). A hoe can't deal with me unless she takes me out; nothing is as critical to her as this. But with gifts – it would be foolish to reject and destabilise what is in principle good Behaviour. The most important issue is that of her being in the frame of mind to be generous and thoughtful. That is a prerequisite to the issue of what she gets me. So, for example, when asked if I'd like a snack in the office, although I have something preferable in my draw, I welcome the opportunity to have a positive interaction and to be able to give her positive feedback. When we are interacting happily because of this, there is the best chance for her to learn and care more about my preferences. In the end, I like a hoe to exclusively buy me items I want. So if she buys me items I don't like, Packaging will address it. I accept the gift, then Reward and encourage her generosity. I communicate my preferences to her at another time. Preferably as near to the time that she selects her next gift as possible.

If I had rejected the offer, or given the impression that I didn't like the gift, then I would have given her less reason to make any effort again, for fear of another negative event.

If it is a choice of either, or, I'd rather have ten gifts than us both wait, and wait, whilst she saves up for a single gift ten times bigger. I don't want my hoe saving up for a prolonged period of time if it affects her usual generosity, and therefore our usual activities will be impacted in the meantime. Plus who knows if we will still be dating ten weeks from now?

I prefer that gifts are handed to me in person, where possible. Transfers, posted cheques and delivered items are harder to Bridge and Reward. In these cases a phone call or correspondence from me to her would be required - and I'm not au fait with making outgoing calls. I don't store my hoe's numbers for any other reason than to identify text messages. But if the above happens then I will use it to show my appreciation and promise (bridge) a Reward.

I prefer to be taken on shopping trips as part of Rendezvous, but secondary credit and charge cards are welcome if offered. I make an effort to understand how much spending with it is sustainable and reasonable for her. My policy is to be sensible and respectful of generosity. I am always considerate of her Potential. Again: moderate and regular is my ethos. I use secondary cards only for everyday expenses that I'd have incurred anyway: food, petrol, toiletries, music and books. I do not purchase luxuries unless invited to.

If asked to contribute towards a card bill that is way within her Potential, I'd say something calmly like, "Drive me to the nearest ATM." Or "Let's go get it. It will be money well spent." I've got more lines than AT&T for these hoes, but going quiet is very effective communication.

A Fox must be independent and not concede Power over his, or her, life. This is the reason why I stated that I would only buy everyday items on a secondary card. Neither will I accept use of a vehicle. If there is a spare vehicle – or spare anything - I don't borrow or loan it, I receive it. I would want it in my name. I say, "It would feel improper to be driving someone else's car. I never go into debt. I wouldn't feel independent. I would like to be able to think of anything I have as mine."

Everything a hoe does for me is fuelled by her desire to reverse the Balance of Power. The need for me to choose her more. To steal the ball and run things on her terms.

By now she will understand better that she can only strengthen our relationship via what she does for us. So there will be occasions when she'll try to use her "ace" to attempt to "Power Bait." A high Potential hoe could be dangling a very juicy offer in front of me, hoping that it throws me off guard. It may smell irresistible. It may be delicious. But the hook planted deep in it will snare me if I snatch the bait like a trick. She'll try to negotiate what she can get, or behave as if she has suddenly bought my life. What I need to be airtight on is that the hoe disables any trap before I take the cheese. Meaning that I only accept an offer if she understands that it carries no implications, no effect on my independence, on the Balance of Power. There is no negotiation, only a spin of the roulette wheel of Wishes will be granted, which I will explain further in the next chapter. There are no strings attached. We all know that a gift by its very nature can't be given in expectation of something in return. That would be a bribe, right? Good Karma brings good Karma, but gifts don't have conditions attached.

Advanced Rewarding

*A hoe's scratch ain't never longer
than a Pimp's cold game.
Pimp, by Iceberg Slim*

Tricks give themselves. Hoes sell themselves. A Fox receives offerings.

Hoes don't give out of sympathy, they give to get, or in the hope of getting. Advanced Rewarding recognises this. They aren't going to part with any waddage or be on their best Behaviour unless they believe that they're buying something with it. Hoes try to buy my ethics, buy the Balance of Power and their Wishes, but when they don't consistently receive as much as they expect, or what they expect, they appreciate any progress.

Perhaps people who regularly spend on the lottery have a similar outlook. They're thinking, "What would I do if..." They are paying or making the effort for the possibility to win. "I have a tiny chance of winning if I enter. But if I don't enter I have no chance." The thrill of participating and receiving small to medium jackpots at unpredictable rates anaesthetises them to the statistics. They get a rush when they win a few pounds.

The positive way I appreciate and encourage Behaviour described earlier is the key to having a considerate, thoughtful, generous hoe who behaves ethically, even thought she would not do if she was allowed to run things. But, over time, she may become more conscious of this consistent consequential way of Rewarding Behaviour. So Advanced Rewarding addresses its four undesirable consequences. First, she could grow bored of the predictable routine: my mystique and the intensity and allure of Rewards will diminish. Second, if she begins to understand, she will be in a better position to test me - it is impossible to control someone you don't understand. Third, it looks contrived. Fourth, a Fox wants to be in control and does not want to be obliged to

Reward things on cue. It should be the Fox who decides if and when they are going to be intimate.

So as soon as Rewarding Behaviour has been effectively established, I move to Advanced Rewarding for that particular Behaviour. By becoming inconsistent in Rewarding it, I prevent anything negative from occurring, increase the Balance of Power and maintain the peace and harmony.

Advanced Rewarding will shake up her Etch-a-Sketch! Instead of Rewarding Behaviour consistently, I emulate a roulette wheel, randomising Rewards. The jackpot is the former standard Reward. The lower value, higher-odd prizes are a variety of lesser Rewards. The most frequent outcome being a no-win. Think about how when we press a wall switch and the light doesn't turn on, our conditioning makes us vigorously flick the switch again and again, before we quit. If I was a dolphin trainer I would use this system by only holding out a fish for the mammal every fifth time that it jumped. However, to ensure it jumped high each and every time, I would also Reward it with fish at random intervals and a variable: a different Reward of equal of lesser value such as new fish, toys, applauding, or playing with the dolphin.

Let's say a Low Clouter regularly brings DVD and tub of ice cream to my home. We watch the film together. Near the end of the film foreplay develops, and we get intimate. We are making the act of watching a new film, that she must supply, and the Reward, a routine. Advanced Rewarding would affect this predictable event by giving it three possible outcomes: on the least number of occasions, giving a higher Reward by interrupting the movie early to be intimate; on many occasions continuing with the established routine; but on the majority of occasions, doing nothing but watch the movie together. I will then Reward the next good deed. This starts to establish that extra effort is needed now and then to make things perfect. It also ensures that I am not being controlled or put on cue. Perhaps I will Reward her when she prepares and brings us drinks from the kitchen. Or when she also brings my dry cleaning with her. Or after the movie when she clears everything up neatly, if she hasn't done it before. By Rewarding Behaviour consistently, I was not able to do this.

In the near future, when I put the previously established Reward for serving drinks on random and wait for something else highly desirable to happen, I've just depolarised her compass! And she's deriving more of a thrill than ever from any Reward she can get. I must always be the source of pristine excitement for a hoe, not through perspiration, but through intellect.

When a given act is followed closely by a reinforcer, the organism tends to increase the frequency of that act under the same or similar conditions.
The Behaviour of Organisms, by Burrhus Skinner

Bolting

Tricks aren't aware there are 3 billion women on earth.
Paradise

A hoe will blow in the wind at anytime. Particularly during the Copping process. The longer I have been hers, the less likely she is to loose touch. Here's why.

From day one, people invest time, effort and money in a relationship. The more they invest, the less likely they are to abandon it. Imagine you have invested heavily in a company. Should the share value dip a little, you are going nowhere. You're going to look on the bright side, look to the future, instead of abandoning your investment. This is why it's essential to allow a girl to express herself and lay down as large a deposit as possible to prove her selection of me ASAP.

True Power stems from having principles. Indifference to a hoe accepting me for who I am, or ceasing Choosing me and Bolting. She could even be my last one or only one. My frame of mind is that I have always gone on to have a better relationship and woman than the last. Another will turn up. Did you know there are three billion women on this planet?

I don't care if tricks would swim upstream in poo just to glimpse her. No matter how beautiful she is, or how outrageous her bank balance is, there are a million more of them. If someone doesn't think that, they should get out more often. In fact, the bad thing about having hoes is that they are time-consuming, and that limits my Clout building and opportunities to meet someone superior. I will never know whom I have missed during the time that I have spent in relationships. So if someone Bolts, I view it as a welcome opportunity to Copp someone superior. I haven't lost anything but a girl who isn't right for me and doesn't meet my standards. And I've gained everything that she's done for me whilst she was mine. She will not have been able to cause any financial or emotional damage or manipulate me. I can't loose. A Fox runs things airtight. A relationship's success is not measured in enjoyment, not time. Did you know movies are better when someone takes you! Food tastes much nicer when it's bought or prepared for you! And I never disliked a someone enough to give back gifts!

A hoe may Bolt for any reason. She could leave merely as the result of testing me out and getting Fired, trying to flip the Balance of Power. Maybe I was too Intimate too soon. Maybe she felt she couldn't compete. Maybe I was so laid back that she thought that she stood no chance with me, or she found a trick who's Clout blew her away. It all boils down to her not Choosing me sufficiently. It will just happen. C'est la vie.

One thing I do care about is learning from experiences. The times I have advanced and grown fastest were through being struck down by masterful hoes. Like Obi-1, they may strike me down, but I will become more Powerful than they could possibly imagine. There wasn't a hoe that could test me I couldn't learn something from, if I paid attention. But I don't loose any sleep thinking if I could have prevented a hoe from Bolting: I'm saying if she was a real pro at testing me, I might analyse and utilise her phrases and methods myself. Assess my own Behaviour and strategies. Incidentally, I should also point out that any aspiring Fox seeking some tuition should get a hoe to coach him. I don't mean by asking her, I mean, for example, if he's not sure how to rebuff a hoe telling him he should pay on a date, he needs to order a hoe to take him out, hold his breath and hit the "record" button in his brain. She's going to dump a lot of useful vocabulary on him! Or show him actions speak louder than words. Either way it's a great lesson.

Hoes will always front and test me from time to time. If she says she's finishing with me, there are no dramatics, it's as simple as that. It's her decision. It's her loss. If she's "unsure" whether she wants to see me, Dr Paradise has an instant cure. I tell her that I understand and it's best we both get on with our lives. I haven't got time for a woman who doesn't know what she wants. See how soon she makes her mind up then.

When Bolting, a hoe wants me to show Emotional Dependency, to trick and try to coax her into staying. They might even express disappointment that I don't break down for them. The majority of hoe's actions are to provoke reactions, my reader. Not for the apparent purpose of the action. They're checking if I've been fronting on them, but I test out under any conditions. Why should they care if I care, if they're going? They're obviously still Choosing, still looking for signs! They're contending for the Balance of Power.

When a hoe lets me know that she's Bolting, we have nothing more to say except "Bye." I'm polite with her, I give her a nonchalant quick farewell. I give the vibe that I'm excited that she's making an opportunity for someone superior, who has what it takes to fill the new vacancy. If they want to mess around, I seize the opportunity to Fire them. I won't waste more than a few seconds on it. To do so would give the wrong impression.

The amusing thing is, out of all the hoes I have dealt with, ninety percent of those who Bolt return with their tail between their legs. In fact I love to Fire hoes, because they return so much nicer, with even more respect, understanding, desire and goodies for me. And it weeds out the time wasters, making my stable more streamlined. They have had that important question in the back of their mind answered conclusively.

I never make contact after we finish. This is an unbreakable rule. A hoe will call up within a few minutes, days or even contact me out of the blue, months later. This month I have had "First Contact" from two hoes that haven't been in touch since last year. When there is a lapse in the fulfilment of their Front or Clout needs, hoes refer back to me. They soon discover there's no one on my level out there. The trick money she's probably tapped into will be of petty compensation. If and when she decides to come back, the attitude I take is why should I audition her again? And she should feel it.

Being a 21st Century Fox is about being in control and therefore able to protect one's financial and emotional status. A hoe must pay a penalty upon her return. This is the ideal time to really make her pull out her purse and invest, or make an extraordinary effort. Put her money where her mouth is. How subtle I am about these matters depends on the Balance of Power. I never forgive and forget. Forgiving is telling someone that sorry is good enough. It provides no deterrent and concedes respect and Power. As with any time a hoe steps out of line, I never accept sex or affection as an apology. And talk is cheap.

"I can't disregard bad things, in the same way that I can't dismiss the nice things you do for me. They are both just as real. I am sensitive to both. You can't undo what's done, or how you've been with me. It has happened and it was a big turnoff. It was insensitive, hurtful, disrespectful. The only way we could move forward is if I was sure that you really would be different with me. If you showed that you genuinely mean what you say and you care that you hurt me."

"I felt disappointed because I had in a sense allowed you close to me and trusted you not to abuse that. I know that I'm complex, deep and sensitive, I only want a woman who can appreciate that. By what you did you showed that you weren't my friend. Now you say all these sweet things, so prove it to me, do something, show me you care, that you mean what you say. In a way I'm afraid of seeing you, because I know that if you were nice with me I'd let you be my friend again."

What do I want? The onus is on her to be accepted by me. I make her aware that I'm unsure about her. That I want her if she is right for me. I tell her that if she was right for me she wouldn't have Bolted or I wouldn't have had to cut her loose. She needs to prove her conviction. Convince me of her words and feelings. That tie is cool. That jacket is cool. Allow her to do something significant to make amends. Say I don't want to talk on the phone and that she should call me back if she wants me to meet her to discuss things. Make it hard for her to get an appointment unless there is a clear promise to be fulfilled during that appointment. Maybe say I'm planning to go shopping when asked what I'm doing on Tuesday. It all goes back to her Wishes and Rewarding Behaviour. Remember how Star one is my company.

The only place you'll find sympathy around here is in a dictionary. Right in-between shit and syphilis.
Unknown American doctor

The squeaky hinge needs replacing, not oil.
Paradise

The Beginning

The unexamined life is not worth living.
Socrates

I view the conclusion of this book on paper as the beginning of its most important function. The value of this work lies not in its pages, but in your mind. Be neither a product of my writings or a product of your environment. I encourage you to question all of the information that surrounds you. But do not seek answers externally.

Paradise

Glossary

Big Issue magazine sold by the homeless.
Bolt a horse running away from its stable or owner.
Check to keep in check.
Copp to obtain a hoe.
Firing an ultimatum, the rejection of which means the termination of a hoe's relationship. [Paradise]
First Contact first communication from a hoe who has Bolted.
Fly fashionable, the height of style, extreme beauty.
Front feigning disinterest or superiority.
G a grand, one thousand.
GP General Practitioner. Doctor.
Gander to look.
Glossy magazine with a gloss cover.
Hoe person who considers material possessions, wealth, status, Clout to be most important. Abbreviation for whore. A person who has relationships of any kind for financial reasons.
J R Hartley fishing expert.
JSA Job Seeker's Allowance. Welfare.
Kingsiza huge penis. [Mr Joshua]
Knock copping another Pimp's hoe.
Laws of Reality truths. [Paradise]
M15 British security service. Military intelligence.
Mack ability to talk someone into virtually anything.
Maintenance contact maintained in-between meeting in person.
Minta a woman in mint physical condition, outstanding physical beauty. **3am Minta** a female of average or below physical beauty.
Paradigm underlying theory, approach, philosophy.
Player person who obtains sex and/or financial gain from others by deception. Not gender specific.
Pounds British currency. £1 is at time of printing roughly equivalent to USA $1.50.
Prat to feign rejection in order to increase desire.
Scratch money.
SOP standard operating procedure. Military terminology.
Stable group of hoes belonging to a Pimp.
Symp person who is sympathetic to a hoe.
Symp Day Valentines Day [The Kidd]
Take To Court to initiate contact. To tell a hoe to make further contact. [The Kidd]
Top Performer a hoe that brings considerable wealth to their Pimp. A hoe that is using the full extent of her **Potential** effort and financial resources that could be used.
Trick any person who rewards another financially for sexual reasons.
Tripping extreme excitement.
Twock taking without owner's consent. A police term.
Waddage wad of notes. Money.

Iceberg Slim
The Lost Interviews
with the Pimp

By Ian Whitaker

**Now available to order worldwide from
amazon.com and amazon.co.uk**

*For orders of two books or more, email us for special
rates: infinitedreamspublishing@gmail.com*

STRAIGHT FROM THE HORSE'S MOUTH: Iceberg Slim gives unprecedented insight into his incredible life as a pimp, when he played God to hundreds of women, in this collection of rare interviews. In his forties Iceberg became a legendary storyteller of another kind. As the USA's best-selling black author he was read by millions. He lectured at colleges, advising students to learn from his mistakes and to lead socially constructive lives. He influenced artists such as Ice-T, Chris Rock, Bill Duke and Jay-Z. In this book Iceberg speaks unflinchingly, sharing his qualified and valuable perspective on important topics: relationships, sex, drugs, racism, crime, prison, politics, family and writing. Inside, Iceberg's fascinating life as a writer, father and husband is also revealed for the first time in exclusive frank interviews with his daughter Misty, and his publisher at Holloway House. These interviews are complimented by rare photos and must-read articles about Iceberg Slim.

"A very complex personality becomes more revealing in Ian Whitaker's engrossing Iceberg Slim: the Lost Interviews. A must read about an era, a culture, an icon of his time."
Bentley Morriss, Holloway House

"Everyone who's read Pimp has a dream that if only they could sit and talk until sunrise with Iceberg... and it would be one of the most fascinating and informative conversations you could ever have. This book is that dream come true! Lost Interviews is the best book I've read this year."
Paradise

"Fine work, seamlessly stitched, provocative and informative. Whitaker uses stories about Robert 'Iceberg Slim' Beck, and interviews, to give us a multi-faceted look at this cultural icon. No judgments are passed, no preaching done, no attempts made to create a devil or a saint. Iceberg Slim, the Lost Interviews makes for a fascinating read. Sensational."
Odie Hawkins

Made in the USA
Middletown, DE
22 June 2023

33235025R00091